The Least One

Marie —

May the joy of the Lord
be yours now + always —

Maureen Hay Read
Nahum 1:7

The Least One

MAUREEN HAY READ

Foreword by Patricia M. St. John

HERALD PRESS
Scottdale, Pennsylvania
Kitchener, Ontario

Library of Congress Cataloging-in-Publication Data

Read, Maureen Hay, 1937-
   The least one / Maureen Hay Read ; foreword by Patricia St. John.
     p. cm.
   ISBN 0-8361-3491-5
   1. Read, Maureen Hay, 1937-   —Diaries. 2. Christian biography-
-United States.   I. Title.
BR1725.R37A3   1989
209'.2'4—dc19
[B]   88-31445
                               CIP

The paper used in this publication meets the minimum requirements of
American National Standard for Information Sciences—Permanence of Paper for
Printed Library Materials, ANSI Z 39.48-1984.

Korean words on cover by Ms. Miok Rho: "the youngest one—dear to
your heart."

THE LEAST ONE
Copyright © 1989 by Herald Press, Scottdale, Pa. 15683
      Published simultaneously in Canada by Herald Press,
      Kitchener, Ont. N2G 4M5. All rights reserved.
Library of Congress Catalog Card Number: 88-31445
International Standard Book Number: 0-8361-3491-5
Printed in the United States of America
Design by Gwen M. Stamm

95 94 93 92 91 90 89 10 9 8 7 6 5 4 3 2 1

*I am not worthy of the least
of all the mercies,
and of all the truth,
which thou hast showed
unto thy servant. . . .*

*Inasmuch as ye have done it
unto one of the least
of these my brethren,
ye have done it unto me.*

—Genesis 32:10; Matthew 25:40

To my dear Ed,
without whom most of this
would not have happened.

Contents

Foreword

The strength and credibility of this story probably springs from the first few pages, for the faith of this writer is no easy, untried faith in a God who blesses his people with loving parents, a happy home, healthy children, and a pleasant environment. Right at the outset, Elizabeth, her only daughter, a four-year-old of rare beauty and promise, dies suddenly of acute meningitis, and from this tragedy the book takes off.

Who can tell what lovely results may grow from a seeming tragedy placed unequivically, with faith and submission, into the hands of God? Who but God could fill the emptiness with a fresh spring of love, flowing out to homeless, abandoned children? Susan from Vietnam and Anne Marie from Korea have taken their places in a singularly happy, united Christian family and Maureen has been enabled to thank God for her three daughters: one safe with the Lord and the other two, still on loan.

This book is not about famous people, nor have the characters any particularly dramatic story to tell. But therein, according to Maureen, lies the real message of the book. "Religious books," she writes, "are mostly about religious or political figures, or those who have undergone dramatic experiences; but what about us ordinary folk, living lives that may be placid, dreary, or colorless? Can Christ give meaning and worth and riches to such? He certainly can and does." And so we read of Grandma, who ran the most welcoming home in the country; and Grandpa, who had just led someone to the Lord "and told in four or five sentences what it would take most people pages to say." We read of Ed, the father with whom they felt safe; of James, who loved all that was old and graceful; of Michael, who liked angels and orchards and saw beautiful things all the time; of Susan, who sat in the woods watching birds; and of Anne, who looked like a bit of peach blossom. Then there is Maureen herself, who yearns to write yet who usually only succeeds in being a busy mother. Yet, in spite of the feminists, she seems to have remained contented with her lot. "Books may soon be forgotten," she writes. "But these children that I am 'writing,' forming line upon line, precept upon precept, are stories that have no end and live forever; how they live depends largely on Ed and me.

These characters are also very real. Like us, they have their ups and downs; their marriage disagreements, depressions, days when everything goes wrong and mother is "worn to a frazzle" with all of them. But through it all there runs that steady recognition of the forgiving, renewing grace of God that shines like light on the small events of every day, making them significant: on flowers, hoarfrost, and clouds, and on the faces of children, making them glowingly beautiful. "Who but God could synchronize such a multitude of music?" she writes of the dawn chorus. Because of that underlying sense of the grace and love of God, small things become precious and memorable and this, to her, is extremely important. "Memories hold a child steady," she wrote. "They are something to remember and miss in the low places of life. They are something to come back to."

So I warmly commend this book of memories to all those who lead ordinary lives; and to those readers whose days are passed in melodrama and excitement I also commend it, for they may find rest in recalling something that may have escaped them: the glory of God that often shines brightest in the ageless, commonplace setting of home and family love.

Patricia M. St. John
Author of *The Tanglewood's Secret*,
Treasures of the Snow, and other books
Canley, Coventry, England

Author's Preface

The publication of *Like a Watered Garden* in 1977 was the accomplishment of a tentative goal I had set in college twenty years earlier, the answer to countless unspoken prayers, the fulfillment of one of my deepest longings. I had not known nor even guessed that the story line of the book would involve the death of our little daughter, nor did I know the friendships it would bring.

For a great host of people read that first book I wrote, lifted as it was from my diary, and many of you wrote to me in response to it. Your letters warmed my heart. They meant that you too were experiencing the same joys and heartaches and inner growth that I was. We had a bond of friendship though we had never met.

One day we shall, and then many things will make sense, many questions will be answered, and our tears will be wiped away.

A common request has been that I write a sequel. It takes time, though, for experiences to accumulate and ripen, and years have gone by. You may even have forgotten that first story—or you may never have read it at all.

Here then in the Prologue is an intense part of that story before you begin the second volume.

Maureen Read
Narvon, Pennsylvania

The Least One

Prologue

I held her tight against me, four-year-old Elizabeth, and murmured endearments as I rocked. How I treasured the moments even as I wondered. She had so seldom complained in her short life and she was certainly never sick. But tonight something was wrong. It must be the neighborhood virus that she had, I told myself. At bedtime she had seemed more tired than usual and her round blue eyes were even larger as I kissed her good night.

Now, an hour later, she had woken crying. When had she ever done that before? She was our healthy one, bypassing the croup, asthma, and fever that often afflicted James and Michael, a year on either side of her.

As I rocked, strange unbidden thoughts came, thoughts about all the hurts and aches in life ahead. Would I be with her in them as I was now? Would I see her married and bearing her own children?

My only daughter. She was all I had dreamed of in a girl, ever since I was one myself. *How* I loved her!

She clung to me as I got up from the chair. And so for the first time in her life, I told her she could sleep with me.

It was the only way I could console her. Ed would sleep in her bed when he came in at eleven from his evening shift at work.

Did orange juice sound good, I asked her. "It sounds good to have you sit by me," she said.

But as I lay beside her, she would not settle. Twisting, turning, she did not relax and sleep. Ed came home and spoke briefly to us, agreeing that she had indeed got a bad case of flu as so many others had. We would just try to get through till morning and then see a doctor.

Her throat hurt, she said, and I got her a Sucret. But still she tossed.

Suddenly she began heaving, throwing up, but there was hardly anything there. I called Ed, who had just gone to sleep. He went downstairs searching for something to settle her stomach.

She was heaving convulsively now.

"I—wish—I—could—sleep," she said, as I picked her up. And then she went limp.

I called Ed sharply, frantically. She was not breathing. He came and competently gave her mouth-to-mouth respiration. (Just one week before he had completed a first-aid course.) He assured me between breaths she would be all right, a strong girl like her. Then why was she so blue and unresponsive?

It must have been forty minutes until the ambulance came. Her face was the color of skim milk—that beautiful, glowing, laughing face. They cut her little pink nightgown off, the one my friend Cherry had made her for Christmas just two months before. They laid her on the floor and did everything in their power to bring her back.

She never returned. Our daughter was in heaven.

• • •

The month before, it had snowed, then rained, making a hard crust over the top. Elizabeth and James had romped outside, enjoying their lurching walk as, with each step, they poised momentarily on the glaze, then fell through.

Michael, two-and-a-half, watching from inside the window, insisted on joining them. It took five minutes to bundle him up in snowsuit, boots-that-were-too-tight, mittens, and he happily went outside to join the other two.

When I looked again, Elizabeth had his hand and was bringing him to the door. He was crying.

"What happened, Elizabeth?" I asked as I gathered him in and yanked off his boots. She explained how he had got on top of the glaze and slid to the bottom of the slope till he hit a tree.

"How did he get back?"

She answered sturdily and with a trace of humor. "I just crunched down to him and he walked back in my crunches."

And in those desolate days after she left us so abruptly, I realized that's what she had done too. Jesus had come for her that February night and she had followed in his crunches, fearlessly, with not even a backward glance.°

I had always sensed instinctively that losing one's child was one of life's deepest hurts, but until the experience was thrust upon me, I did not know the loneliness and depression that follow. My faith seemed barren, empty. How could anyone say so glibly that all things work to-

---

° It was a virulent form of encephalitis, the Atlanta Center for Disease Control said months later, but Ed and I thought it was probably Reye's Syndrome, prevalent that winter.

gether for good? Did anyone really *know*? Why should *my* little girl be taken, mine who was so winsome and intelligent and happy, who was loved so deeply? Why not some unwanted child?

It is hard to follow the Shepherd when your eyes are full of tears.

Grief seems to get worse for a long time. After the funeral, all I could think of was that grave and her lovely girl-face sagging, crumbling. O death, there is a sting! Doubt snapped at my heels. *What if* I never saw her again? Was God really good? How many times I had held her and told her that I loved her, that she was my only little girl.

Take now thy son, thine only son, whom thou lovest.... This was the word given to Abraham. At the last he was spared.

But another Father wasn't. Through all the eons of eternity, God knew his beloved Son would one day die in torment for the sins of the world. For me. Why had he even created the world when he knew such a price would have to be paid? There had to be some hidden meaning to all sin and suffering that God thought it worthwhile to proceed, to go ahead and make the world, knowing all the while the immeasurable cost of redemption. There must be something that none of us in this life can see or understand, something which will one day make sense.

Not that I thought all this out logically, but as grim months passed, and the ache was still there, I learned to *trust* him. I had to. *Lord, to whom shall we go? Thou hast the words of eternal life.*

Quite simply, there was no hope, no joy, no point to anything apart from Christ. *Lord, I believe. Help thou my unbelief.*

And that's when he came to me and I began walking in his crunches again.

• • •

As time passed, a childhood dream of mine surfaced, a longing to adopt a child, a daughter. When I mentioned it diffidently to Ed, he seemed willing enough, admitting we *needed* a girl.

Dreams are sometimes costly. Never in my early youthful hopes had I thought of the dark road we would travel that led us now to adoption. The ways of God are past finding out.

In March 1975, a year after Elizabeth's death, I began to attend a series of nine meetings at the home of Barb Tremitiere, mother of thirteen, in York, Pennsylvania, fifty miles away. Ed, because of work, was able to go to just three. We filled out long forms and paid various fees. There was to be a waiting period of from six to ten months for a Korean child.

But the war in Vietnam was rapidly ending that spring of 1975. In all that debacle, hundreds of children were airlifted from Saigon and all the world watched, including us. There was something heart-catching to see planeloads of waifs arriving in the United States.

One April night at 11:00 p.m. Barb phoned. Would we be ready to take a little Vietnamese girl, age five, *tomorrow*? I gasped. Oh, we were, of course, we were.

As Ed came in from work, I rushed to tell him, laughing and crying all at once. I couldn't sleep and sat a long time alone in the living room. This new little girl, where were her parents? Was she afraid? What heartache had she known? Along with these questions were memories of Elizabeth, anticipation, and grief all mingled and intertwined into a sob.

The next morning I woke at six and scampered across the road to tell my folks, who had prayed with us. Dad was at the kitchen table. He choked up when I told him, then called Mom to hear the news.

After a rather distracted (on my part) birthday party for Michael, who had just turned four, we left for York to pick up our new daughter. On the way we shopped at Good's. I loved buying girl's clothes again, practical things mostly, and one pink frilly dress for church. That was for me as much as her. I was by fits ecstatic and aching.

At the Tressler headquarters we saw them arrive, a vanload of children, all coming to *parents* for the first time. A dear little girl was handed to me and we sat and cried together. Susan Joy Dinh Read.

She was adorable, mischievous, hilarious, endlessly energetic. She soon learned English, picked strawberries, cried with homesickness, fought with the boys, charmed Ed. There were strains and joys over the next months, but never did we look back. Susan was ours in a profound way.

I often looked at her in bed at night, the smooth brown skin, her lovely almond-shaped eyes closed tightly in sleep, and wondered if anyone had ever hovered over her before, smoothing her hair, touching her, praying for her, all the motherly things one takes for granted. Was her mother alive? Did she ever think of her, ache to see her?

One night about a year later, we sat at bedtime and talked. Susan asked if her skin would be white in heaven. I assured her she was a dear little brown girl and doubtless would be in heaven too, that Jesus liked her just the way she was. She looked relieved.

Then, would she like a brown sister? In the dim light we talked, her dark eyes shining with expectation.

We began to pray, just us two, for a sister. I didn't dare tell Ed. It was an outlandish thing to do, considering how cramped we were in our small house. Why then were we praying for another? Where would we even put her? Could we afford it? How could we change the mind of Ed, who thought we had enough? Does God really *answer* prayer?

This book is the story of that prayer—and the answer.

Faith

---

*Without faith it is impossible to please
him. . . . Lord, increase our faith.*

It began as a little seed-prayer, soon after Susan, our
Vietnamese daughter, came in 1975. She wanted another
little girl, a brown one just like her. We began, together, to
pray for one. Fervent at first, our faith waned, wilted, and
sometimes almost disappeared. But the box of little girl's
clothes that we kept in the crowded closet upstairs was a
tangible symbol, a reminder, of the hidden prayer in our
hearts.

Prayer—is it any more than a dream given over to God
in faith to let him fulfill as he chooses? And while we
waited for that little girl for the next six years and more,
God gave us other answers to dream-prayers: big ones like
the publication of my first book, a memorable trip to the
British Isles, and small ones like—but when you read, you
can find them for yourself. . . .

Chapter

1

March 17, 1977

Adoption—it was a dream of mine when I was a little girl, to one day have children who were "left over," whether through death, neglect, whatever.

Today the dream became legally true. After having Susan for two years, she became ours officially as Judge Appel declared us the parents of Susan Joy Dinh Read.

The courtroom, austere and somber, gave us a sense of awe and, yes, fear, as we stood before the judge and answered questions. I stumbled when he asked me how much money Ed earns in a year. Such facts don't stick to me, but Ed prompted me, and I saw a glint in the judge's eye. At the end he did smile broadly and congratulated us. It was so legal, yet so moving.

Afterward we went to McDonald's. When we first got Susan in York two years ago, it was there that she stopped crying and smiled at us for the first time. It seemed fitting to go today.

Later at the foot of the Narvon Hill Ed dropped us off and went on to another errand. We walked home, the children frisking like lambs let out to pasture. It was one of those limpid early spring evenings with grass greening, water chuckling in little creeklets by the side of the road, crocuses blooming here and there.

Susan is ours forever. Walking home, I thought of how God had chosen us before the foundation of the world to be adopted by Jesus Christ to himself. We are his forever, too, and it was appointed before the world was built. To think that God thought of me way back then.

Susan and I are praying now for that other little one to come. Another daughter and a bigger house, it says on my prayer list. I wonder when or how God will work it out.

May 30, 1977

Susan—how much she has learned—and taught me also. For two years now we've been trying to stop her nail-biting. It was compulsive and done so neatly and efficiently that I scarcely ever saw her do it. I tried cajoling, threatening, some ill-tasting stuff, none of which worked.

Recently she began to pray that God would help her stop biting her nails. He did. They're longer than they've ever been with all my strategies. When I queried her, she said, "Jesus tells me in my heart not to do it." Faith can move mountains and grow fingernails.

June 4, 1977

I've seen the galleys for *Like a Watered Garden*. Can it be? Me, the author of a book? The whole thing is beginning to hit me a little more, my twenty-year dream to write a book coming true.

As I read it, I was pleasantly surprised that Paul Schrock did scarcely any editing on it.

Yet I have doubts and deep fears at times. Will Ed like it? Are the few references to his mother kind though humorous? What will his family say? For that matter, what will mine say?

I made some hard choices in what was included, what was left out. Were they right choices? It's scary at this stage, on the eve of publication.

I pray daily that God will filter through each page and use it. *Not unto us, O Lord, not unto us, but unto thy name give glory.*

July 1, 1977

This morning Susan, eight today, was at the post office next door looking for birthday cards. She came home with a box of a dozen copies of *Like a Watered Garden.* In the midst of housecleaning the boys' room, I happened to be outside hanging up sheets, bedspreads, and blankets under blue sky, loving the feel of summer warmth, when she rushed to tell me.

Almost too busy to feel elation, I noticed my gut reaction, the loss of appetite that always attends me when I am extremely tense, sad, or joyful. There was probably some of all three—a certain tension over the reactions of folk, those near and dear to me, trembling joy and excitement because a dream so long desired was fulfilled, and a heaviness at the thought of the cost of the dream. Elizabeth's untimely death is what gives the book depth and poignance. How I pray that it will touch and cheer and help many, to give beauty for ashes, the oil of joy for mourning, the garment of praise for the spirit of heaviness.

That is my prayer, but the deepest reaction this morning was a certain fear and ache.

July 30, 1977

O Lord, I am oppressed. Undertake for me. Thus prayed Hezekiah and so do I. In spite of the fun and glory of the book, I am oppressed these days. Marital tension completely undoes me.

We trekked out to Missouri for a couple weeks, my first time there without Grandma Read. I felt an unexpected sadness at the strangely unhappy life she had lived, at the miseries she and I felt when we lived there together, and an acute sense of Ed's loss since she left last January. Perhaps that loss accounts even for some of our present friction.

O Lord, undertake for us.

August 22, 1977

Forty years old. I couldn't possibly forget the fact with so many people reminding me. Ed took us all out to dinner at Zinn's, where we dined sumptuously and spent half a week's worth of grocery money on one meal. It is a tradition for him to treat us on my birthday and I always accept gladly!

In the evening Mom and Dad invited us for tea and gave me forty dollars tucked inside a book by Gordon Mc-Donald. The McConaghays came, later Aunt Sadie and Aunt Ruth, Russ and his family. A happy evening. Is there any joy greater than being with one's family and friends?

... *these forty years the Lord thy God hath been with thee; thou hast lacked nothing.* Not one single thing, Lord. Thank you.

August 24, 1977

Today Susan got mad at me as she is wont to do when

rebuked. She won't go and pout in a corner, oh no. She stays underfoot and gives me baleful looks with her dark eyes and does annoying things like holding the refrigerator door open so that I'll yell again and get more upset. This can go on for hours. I've tried many tactics—punishment, silence, lectures, none of which are all that successful. However, I managed to unsettle her today. After my pickles were canned, I jumped into the car and went shopping at Good's, leaving her with Ed and the boys. She hates to be left behind. When I got back, she was friendly again.

At bedtime I read again from Patricia St. John's *Treasures of the Snow* to the youngsters. It's a lovely story of forgiveness, not holding grudges, confessing easily, loving one another. We talked about it together. Then as she got into bed, Susan came and whispered to me, "I'm sorry I didn't talk to you today." This was the first time that she ever apologized.

September 20, 1977

How thoroughly God takes care of us, of me. I had worried about too many responsibilities at school this year. It turned out that no one *wanted* journalism, which took care of the time an extra course would require and demolished my ego as well (me an author and all), probably what God intended. Then one of the mothers, an exquisitely beautiful and talented woman, volunteered to help with the Christmas play, my other big concern. The Lord's sense of humor shows at times like this. She will obviously upstage me, which I should have gotten used to a long time ago, but one always needs to be reminded of one's limitations.

Probably the hardest setback is having younger children

as my chief responsibility in our ACE program. I, who always had high school, find I must change gears considerably. It has been, well, humiliating to take a "lower place." Thus I have grades 4-6, a group that I'm learning to love. They are old enough not to need their shoes tied and noses wiped, yet young enough to believe what I tell them.

October 2, 1977

When I actually come right down to choosing, Aunt Sadie has probably been my favorite aunt. Certainly she was the one with whom I spent the most time. As a small child I adored her simply because she adored me. I remember her taking Russell and me to the creek on hot days to wade and build dams. Then we went on to the barn to jump in the hay, shrieking and giggling and raising a cloud of dust. I remember stopping there every single day as I walked home from school to see her and Granny Russell. I always stayed as long as I could, sometimes longer than I should have, and stuffed myself with candy and pretzels.

As I grew older, I began to realize that Aunt Sadie had somehow missed her calling, that all the love she lavished on me should have been given to the daughter she never had. Being a shy, plain, easygoing woman, she had stayed home for years and cared for parents who were infirm. When they died, it was too late to do anything else. Besides, Ruth and George, also unmarried and working, needed someone at home to cook and wash their clothes.

I loved her dearly, but I pitied her too as I grew up, with that condescending pity the young often feel for their elders. But as time went on, the pity became respect for her unbounded kindness and her love for me. Her health declined, and a year ago she broke her hip. Yet her sense of humor persisted and she seemed cheerful.

Which is why it was such a heartbreaking shock today when Aunt Ruth found her on the kitchen floor early this morning with her face in a pan of water and a note on the table. How could anyone as gentle and indecisive as she do something so violent and single-minded? The note was old. Perhaps this had been on her mind for years.

I am horrified and numb with grief. How could I have loved someone all my life and not *known* her?

Yesterday I nearly invited both aunts for dinner today but felt such exhaustion that I just didn't.

What if I had? Would it have made a difference?

October 14, 1977

It is two weeks since Aunt Sadie died. Nights have been long. Suicide, like nearly all tragedies of life, is not truly felt till one comes close to it.

For example, I never knew how many regrets I would feel. I never knew I would remember the times when I was bored with her illnesses, when I didn't listen as much as I could have or at least not with understanding, when I wished she wouldn't talk so long on the phone just when I had poured a cup of hot tea and wanted to relax.

I never imagined I'd wonder about her eternal state. What if Aunt Sadie were not in heaven? What if she went on being lonely and feeling odd and left out and unloved— forever? The thought is insupportable.

In her note she said she had always longed to be married. I *knew* that with a kind of sixth sense, yet neither I nor anyone else ever talked to her about it. Why were we so reserved, as though it were indecent to mention such things to a maiden lady? Why did it never occur to us that she might love someone? Why did no one ever think she could be exploding at times with anger, passion, love, maybe hate? Our manner was to talk to her about food, cleaning house, the chiropractor, thinking that anything of greater import was beyond her.

Aunt Sadie feared and loved God. I pray that his mercy, which is surely so much greater than mine, has carried Aunt Sadie straight to that home where every unfulfilled dream and whispered prayer comes true. May all she ever longed for be hers now.

November 5, 1977

Ed has decided to go into chimney sweeping. It required a loan, so I was doubtful. But I hope it will be worthwhile. With the price of energy and the widespread return to stoves, there is a need for sweeps.

He's been on ten hours at the mine recently, working till 2:00 a.m., a dreary hour to be abroad and a disturbing one for me. I always awaken when he comes in. Then, having got my first deep sleep over, I sometimes cannot get back to sleep again till four or five. Rising time at six comes all too soon. Oh, for a night of unbroken sleep. Sigh.

November 15, 1977

James had been told to go outside and do a job. He loitered in his bedroom, in no hurry to get to work.

"James, get your clothes changed and get outside," I barked at him. He quietly did as he was told, though his eyes looked a bit red around the rims.

An hour later he sat at the table drinking cider and munching a pretzel. I put my arms around his shoulders, gave him a squeeze, and said, "Thanks, James, for doing a good job. And—I'm sorry I yelled at you so sharply."

He shrugged. "Did you yell? I don't remember." And smiling a little, he kept on munching.

As I went on with dinner preparations, I thought of God's forgiveness. He says that he doesn't even remember our sins, that they are buried in the depths of the sea, that they are as far as the east is from the west.

If he forgets them, I should too.

December 10, 1977

On December 2, Ed and I celebrated our tenth an-niversary. Can it be? How much we have.

Over Thanksgiving weekend we all went amid falling snow to New York City. Ed let me drive (he hates cities), and I loved every minute of it, proving to myself I could still get around in Manhattan.

After spending what seemed hours waiting in a long, cold line, we sailed to the Statue of Liberty, my first visit to the island, though I've been past it many times on ships and planes. With our little alien, it seemed a fitting place to see, and I thought again how this country has received millions of homesick, frightened people (one of them my dad) and welded them into one nation under God. God, bless America.

We hadn't eaten a bite since early morning. When we discovered that it was by then nearly 3:00 p.m., we went ravenously to Chinatown. There we had our first full Chinese meal, each of us ordering something different, consuming copious amounts of food and tea. Only fourteen dollars' worth and we were stuffed, a real bargain in the Big Apple. Muddling about town, giving Ed some more gray hair, we finally got to our hotel, probably the most exciting part for the kids. They love places where we "live" away from home.

Radio City Music Hall (*Pete's Dragon*), the World Trade Center, the port, nostalgic for me with memories of our trip to Ireland in 1951, and on the way home the most horrendous traffic jam I've ever seen. We learned since that more people travel on Thanksgiving weekend than any other. I believe it.

Now there is Christmas to think of with the usual delights of wrapping gifts, baking, preparing for the family dinner to be held here. And yet, there is a big ache when I think of Aunt Sadie. I've missed her. Aunt Ruth, alone in her house now, has her Christmas decorations up and it seems so utterly pathetic.

On the radio tonight I heard part of the matchless *Messiah*, "Since by man came death, by man came also the resurrection." And it began at Christmas.

January 16, 1978

We, the Reads, actually got a *new* piece of furniture. Mostly we seem to gather to ourselves odd bits and pieces from Mom's attic or secondhand shops. This, a spanking new desk, came to replace the old kitchen table Aunt Margaret had set up housekeeping with probably forty years ago, which had been our desk heretofore.

On it is our new typewriter, purchased recently to replace Ed's vintage IBM one, which nearly drove me to such foolishness as kicking or screaming when I typed my book manuscript. So we felt quite dressed up for Christmas with our new furniture in the dining room. I set a plant on it, since removed to make room for all the heaps of letters, a jar of pencils-and-other-useful-items, books, a stack of magazines, a couple hundred newspaper clippings and ads, and such.

This month Elizabeth would be eight years old. She's been gone now as long as ever she was here.

March 20, 1978

What a long winter it's been, though now we see light at the end of the tunnel. Actually it's mud, not light. I blew up at the kids for getting so wet and dirty, then bawled over Michael's face and memories of another little face that looked so like his.

March is simply too much—too much wind, too much brown barreness, thaw, mud, puddles. Yet it is wonderfully exhilarating when one wakens in the morning to daylight and birds and little streams of water giggling along the side of the road.

I've been reading a book on the crucifixion that has moved me to tears. As I get older, the Easter season becomes richer with the depth of love expressed for me and for all who call upon him. He is not willing that any should perish.

I have set myself a kind of fast which is almost funny in its lack of sacrifice. I do not eat after supper in the evenings as I like to do. When I think of food, I remember to pray then for two whom I love dearly that they might have the joy of the Lord, that most priceless gift of God.

April 29, 1978

Yesterday, at the tired end of the school day, a most exciting phone call came from an editor at *Guideposts*, Gary Sledge, speaking for Arthur Gordon. He said marvelous things: that my book brought a tear to his eye, that *Guideposts* is in touch with Paul Schrock about mass-marketing it, that I am invited to a writers' workshop in Rye, New York, with all expenses paid (including airfare), needing only to submit a story for that.

I walked on air all evening. To think that my little quiet book would move a New York editor is one of those exceeding-abundantly-above-all things that God does.

And now I am sitting at our desk looking west at the sun setting behind this lovely tree line, soft with fragile new leaves. The old dead cherry tree has a single live branch with blossoms as white as last month's snow upon it. Birds are making their sleepy sounds. After the orneriest winter in memory, spring has arrived. The children have frisked outside all day and the quiet inside is delightful.

This morning at 5:30 I read in *Daily Light*, "These forty years hath the Lord led thee." He has indeed.

May 15, 1978

The annual week of rain in May, though both ends were laced with sunshine and the splendor of dogwood.

On her Mother's Day card Susan had written, "I love you mom because you send me to this school. I am glad that you adoped [sic] me."

I'm glad too. What would we do without her?

It is strangely quiet at Narvon. Ed flew yesterday to Missouri, his spring pilgrimage to visit friends and work at the farm. Even though it is rented, there are jobs to do. He loves to dig dock and talk about the weather with Don Probert. It's good for him.

And Mom and Dad are away visiting for a long weekend, so the big house across the road is dark.

July 6, 1978

These days are well-nigh perfect, the kind you want to hold in your hand and touch and sniff and *keep*, but instead they are like a wispy dandelion fluff that, when you look at and analyze, is gone. Perfect roses, blue sky, energetic garden. Midsummer.

The kids are so special. I sometimes wish I could tell them what they mean to me. Instead, I tell the Father and commit them again to his care, the only sure refuge.

Susan is nine. Usually I can manage only one birthday guest at a time, but nine is the magic number at our house for a "big" party. This year Susan celebrated with five little girls here to eat lasagna. Dorine stayed overnight.

The next day Ed and I tore up the kitchen to put new floor covering down. We worked together beautifully the whole weekend, he very hard indeed.

Then he built me a picnic table and benches, painted them the color of redwood, and now we are having dinner outside each day under the tree at noon. Everyone waves at us as they go by—it's a bit public—but then, why not? We must look very happy gnawing on chicken legs, licking our fingers, throwing bones to Spot, eating raspberries and ice cream. Folks smile and we smile back.

It would be wonderful to have another little girl.

July 9, 1978

This spring we saw a pair of Canada wild geese that appeared to be staying in Ronnie Fox's meadow below us. Their honking and flapping drew our attention. No matter how many geese flew overhead, these remained where they were, unperturbed by any call of the wild. They are still there.

It seemed strange that birds of such independence would live on a small field with sheep, ducks, and chickens, even if there was food and safety.

"Geese mate for life," said Ed one day.

That's nice, I thought idly. Better than many people manage.

Recently he made another observation. "The female goose over there has a broken wing. She can't fly."

"She can't?" I said. "Then that explains why they are here. Her mate won't leave her, not even when other flocks go by and call for him."

Ed nodded. "For better or worse, he's with her."

I like that. Loyalty.

Loyalty to a spouse, to a handicapped child, to an ailing parent, to a friend in trouble, loyalty in any relationship is the part of love that never fails.

July 27, 1978

It was the first really big (meaning expensive) vacation we've ever had. We flew west, spending ten days mostly in Ouray, Colorado, with Ed's cousins, the Clousers. We walked and swam and went horseback riding, a first for me, though Ed said I looked like I'd been doing it all my life—kind man! I was sore for days after.

In the middle we drove in a rented car to the Grand Canyon, which must be seen to be believed; Mesa Verde, the quaint stone cliff Indian villages; the Painted Desert; and through miles of wild, dramatic country that is a sharp contrast to lush Lancaster County.

Returning, I wondered if Uncle Bob would yet be alive. Having worked with asbestos so many years at work, he is now in the breathless vise of lung disease.

Yet he was here when we got back, his brown eyes shining with delight to see us again. Dad's only brother in this country, he has always been a favorite uncle of ours. In this last dreadful illness, he seems to have drawn very near to God and his tongue is loosed. He can express his faith. It is a special comfort to me that he has read my book twice. Did it help to make Christ more real to him?

September 13, 1978

Recently I noticed that nine-year-old James often says to me in the middle of a story, "Mom, are you listening?" Whenever he asked, I wasn't.

It occurred to me that I would never treat a guest in this way. To have my mind planning the next meal or thinking through a reading lesson when someone is talking to me is the height of rudeness. I am busy, yes, but if something must be scratched from my schedule, it should not be moments with my children. Surely they, of all people, deserve some uninterrupted, full concentration time.

Thus was born the tea hour. Once a week I spend an hour alone with each one, usually after supper. We sit at the kitchen table with cups of tea (not too strong and with lots of milk in it for them), a nice dessert, or maybe a piece of scone with butter and jam, and we talk. I try to listen mostly.

The other two youngsters read, listen to records, or play in the next room.

I am touched at how much each one looks forward to it. James shows me pictures of ships and faraway places. He has an abiding interest in things old and beautiful. Susan will tell me about the ball she caught in school or a bird she saw. She has wonderfully sharp observation powers and will sit at length in the woods to watch. Michael, always a bit whimsical, might suggest there are lions living in the basement and we surmise about that. Or we'll look at a *World Book* together.

These are golden hours, priceless, and once gone, irretrievable.

September 27, 1978

It was quite a week at Rye, New York, with the *Guideposts* staff and guest speakers. At the airport I was met by Van Varner and Bill Deerfield and whisked off with fourteen other workshoppers from all over the country to a lovely old mansion called Wainwright House in Rye. It overlooked Long Island Sound with New York City twenty miles in the distance.

I shook hands and talked with the likes of Norman and Ruth Peale, Arthur Gordon, John and Elizabeth Sherrill (a favorite), Catherine Marshall, Marjorie Holmes, and others. It was invigorating, to say the least.

Overwhelming too. Though we were honored guests and our work treated with respect, I felt out of my league.

For one thing, my clothes seemed dowdy. New Yorkers are always a season or two ahead of us, or rather, I suppose we are behind. And I lack self-confidence when I'm with urbane, sophisticated folk, though why I should, I don't know. In Christ I am complete and as the *Living Bible* puts it, nothing can be added to completeness.

The final evening was to be a night on the town, eating at a restaurant and attending a play, all at *Guideposts* expense, as indeed the whole week had been. However, my heart won over my social instinct and I opted to fly home to my hubby and three little ones. Actually, I was homesick by that time. Jean Bell Mosley from Missouri, another country girl at heart, did likewise and we left together in a kind of cheerful relief to be going home.

The hard part remains, writing something that *Guideposts* can use, a tall order.

October 7, 1978

It was one of those incomparable October days when the wind whipped the clothes, snapping them crisply on the line and making even the bathroom smell fresh when I put the clean towels back on the racks. Hanging clothes outside on such a day as this is one of my favorite housewifely tasks.

The garden is full of leftovers. Gaunt, aged zinnias glow with astonishing brilliance here and there, like embers of a dying summer. The persistent cherry tomatoes still adorn my salads but the cucumbers have succumbed to gross overweight.

And now this evening little Michael (is he really seven?) came prancing from his bath with his red-striped pajamas, the buttons cockeyed making one side hang lower, a front tooth missing, his hair dripping, and his smile angelic, wanting to be read to. What did I do to deserve him?

Recently, when I was cleaning the kitchen, he suggested we rearrange it. That's hard to do in our limited space, I told him. "Maybe we could rearrange the wastebaskets," he said. And we did.

October 9, 1978

Just now James fell hard on the sidewalk outside. I heard him crying, sobbing, something he's not done for awhile.

I thought of all the times he'll cry, or wish he could, over a thousand hurts worse than that one. Most of them I'll never know.

October 17, 1978

When I got home from school, there was a longer-than-usual note from Ed, who had gone to work. Was he upset about something? I can't bear misunderstandings. Instead, he reported a phone call from *Guideposts*, which will publish 200,000 copies of my book. Since it is small, it will be printed in a volume with one by Charles Allen.

I'm ecstatic and deeply grateful to God. Only he could have done this for such a simple, homely story.

I had read that wonderful classic recently—S. D. Gordon's *Quiet Talks on Prayer*—and I had committed the whole thing to God. Tonight I can hardly contain all I feel about his leading again. *The Lord shall guide thee continually.*

Right now I'm listening to Christmas carols on the stereo. It's that kind of evening.

October 22, 1978

On Friday Betty Ann phoned collect, which meant something was terribly amiss, and said her husband had walked out on her for another woman. I was heartsick, but not overly shocked, having found him strained and unfriendly at Rea and Derrick's last week.

Ed was at work, so I left the children with Mom and went over immediately. She was completely distraught, almost irrational, and I feared for her mental and physical well-being. Betty Ann has always adored him, more than he deserved, I used to think. He seemed to truly love her, at least until lately when something seemed out of joint.

For Betty Ann, it is the end of her very purpose for living. She loves God dearly but this seems almost more than she can bear.

I spent last night with her. This morning, driving home early in the Sunday stillness with mist in the valleys and jeweled leaves, the loveliest day of autumn, I wondered again how life can be so hard at times. This is my first closeup of a broken marriage, and it's one of the ugliest sights I can think of.

I came home and kissed my dear hubby, thankful again for his sturdy faithfulness. A stable godly home is probably the greatest gift one can have. Our children are wealthy and so am I.

November 22, 1978

Tomorrow is Thanksgiving, the first one I can remember that Mom isn't here to cook for us. Her specialties are sweet potatoes that drip with brown sugar and butter and turnips done to a turn with bits of bacon. She came dangerously close to a devastating stroke a few weeks ago and is in the hospital, where she received a pacemaker. The big house across the road looks so empty and feels even worse when you walk in, like a death. Mom has hardly ever not *been* there.

Thus I have the dinner for the clan, but it's a vanishing generation. Uncle Bob is sick unto death, gasping for breath and just a bundle of bones. Aunt Margaret has him lying in their living room, where his face still lights up when anyone walks in. He has fought courageously, but the end must be near now. That he won't die in an agony of suffocation has been a daily prayer. The dinner will be rather somber tomorrow.

Tonight the children helped make the cranberry salad and the dressing. I read them a chapter from *Heidi*, we prayed, and now they're in bed.

It's always easy to thank God for those gifts of his that are agreeable—health, happiness, abundance—but it is much harder to receive gladly those things that are for our learning: illness to teach us patience, loneliness to make us lean hard on him, inconvenience and changed plans to help us rejoice in the Lord, who never changes.

November 30, 1978

The call came this evening that Uncle Bob is gone. My first question was "how," and the answer came—peacefully. Perhaps an angel came and lifted him away, he went so easily. Aunt Margaret was in the kitchen making him a poached egg. When she came back into the room, moments later, he was gone.

Their neighbor, a devout Irish Catholic, has been their mainstay. Each day she helped bathe him and was in and out, always cheerful and talkative. She and Uncle Bob loved each other, the usual bitter animosity of Irish Catholics and Protestants forgotten. There are many contradictions in life, strange mixtures of compassion and indifference, of love for individuals and yet hatred for a group of the same or like individuals. Who could ever sort it out? I'm glad God sees not as man does. He looks at the heart.

I can hardly believe that all the years with Uncle Bob are over—and I had so *many* happy times. How often I spent the night in their elegant home when I was just a "wee girl," as he called me. There were always crowds of Irish people, big teas, polished hardwood floors, a lovely sun porch, just an aura of luxury. Though he loved children dearly, he never had any, instead lavishing his affection on his nieces and nephews.

We shall miss him sorely.

December 11, 1978

Christmas cards are arriving these days and we hang them at the foot of the stairs. They look so festive.

The cards, however bright, do not contain all happy news. Aunt Margaret is desperately lonely without Uncle Bob. She had cared for him night and day for so long that she is floundering now. Then I learned today the marriage of a friend in Boyertown has dissolved after thirty-four years. That is the third one in two months among my friends. What is *happening?* The fabric of our country is unraveling and all that is safe and precious falling through: security, loyalty, patience, kindness, courtesy, love, those things of which a home is made.

Betty Ann is desolate, no job at present, her kids back in their own homes again, and she's alone. Her twenty-second wedding anniversary is this month, only there's nothing to celebrate. This is happening to good people, godly people, and one hardly knows how to handle it. *How* does one help a life that has exploded emotionally?

Three things come to mind:

I can refrain from judging why it happened. These women worked as hard at their marriages as I do mine, maybe harder.

I can listen to their heartaches and keep them to myself.

I can pray for them, regularly, specifically, earnestly.

January 8, 1979

Today four of the five devotionals that I had sent to

Guideposts came back. I can't quite seem to swing it with them. Who can know the mind of an editor?

At times like this, I have self-doubts. Am I to go on writing? It is such an effort. Is my ambition simply ego-inspired or does God want me to write? It may be just a conceit, a desire for self-gratification at the expense of other better things, a vanity of vanities, as the Preacher says in Ecclesiastes. Of the making of books there is no end. There is not much point in adding another second- or third-rate book to the multitude already on the marketplace. Thus I reason.

And then this evening I read from Ezekiel, the opening chapters of his amazing vision of God. I need always to come back to that to get a true perspective. Who am I that he should think to use me? Yet he has, he does, he *will*.

January 10, 1979

Tea with Michael. Such a cozy little boy he is, snuggling close to look at books. He told me he likes angels and thinks about them a lot. He imagines a lamb lost at sunset and an angel finds it. Tonight he confided that he likes orchards too—they sound nice. And indeed they do, now that I think of it. He would have liked my Granny Russell's, just a small friendly orchard near the big willow tree with an odd chicken or two wandering here and there under the trees.

He sees beautiful things all the time: sky, the wind blowing in the trees, sunsets, light shining through clouds. And one of his chief pleasures on a warmish day is to climb the hemlock tree clear to the top, a dizzy height, and sing loudly, "O beautiful for spacious skies, for amber waves of grain. . . ."

I hope he will always climb high and sing and love orchards and angels. A boy can't go far wrong doing that.

January 25, 1979

Today Elizabeth would be nine. It's been a hard day, backache, grocery shopping after school with three hungry scrappy kids in tow, then a turbulent evening. Little Leslie Wilson came to stay awhile, and he, with my three, seemed to do everything they shouldn't do in the house: gymnastics, hide-and-seek, climbing all over the furniture. When his mom called and said she was going out, I told her to get him right away. I knew from experience we could have him all night if she went away.

Then a parent phoned about his child, one of my students, while I was having tea with Michael. As we talked, James and Susan began to fight noisily. After I swatted them, I nearly bawled on the phone.

Now they're using one of their two weekly TV hours at Mom's. I hugged them, then cried after they left.

This is a low time of year, memories, weather, a crowded, cluttered house.

And to think Susan and I are praying for another child.

March 14, 1979

As I left school to go shopping, in the cloudless beauty I thanked God that I was working there at Twin Valley these years where I firmly believe God placed me; that I have good health; that I can teach and influence young people in ways that matter; that my children, our own three, are with me daily, and I need not trouble, yet at least, about those sinister sins that prey on youngsters; that I have a dear hubby who works and buys groceries for us; that I can

53

honorably write a check for them and bring home a car loaded with food for another week.

Ed is excited about a project that he hopes will make us prosperous. Actually, we are right now.

March 15, 1979

Michael, practicing piano, got upset with Susan. His tears are strangely touching always.

Just now I've taken them across the road to watch television for an hour at Mom's. Cold night, clear black sky with starpoints of light. O Lord, are you *really* there? Do you care? Doubts. Will we ever be rid of them altogether until we see him? I get so hungry to *know*, to see him. "Now we see through a glass, darkly; but then face to face." There are times, like now, when I can hardly wait.

March 27, 1979

Was there ever a child who ate such unlikely breakfasts? All the leftovers Susan hides in the back of the refrigerator, then heats them the next morning: stew, rice, chicken, spaghetti, and today sauerkraut, which she also packed into her thermos for lunch. Half the school sniffed it while she ate. With her remarkable self-discipline, she still eats no sweets at all, a big plus.

James—I seem to pick at him lately, partly because I often sense Ed's impatience. James goes on about cathedrals, faraway places, history, books, none of which interests Ed, who likes newspapers, magazines, business mortgages, banks, and such. Yet a child's bent cannot really be changed, should not in fact, or one can mar that which is the real person and twist out of shape what God intended.

James has an inquiring mind, a good mind, and reads voraciously. He talks constantly and all I do is give him a listening ear.

There is such a fine line in letting a child pursue his interests and yet guiding him. James cannot be aimless, but he must not be forced into a mold. Ed and I both need wisdom, he not to be intolerant, and I not to be weak. It's that wisdom that is from above which we need, a wonderful blend of discernment, patience, kindness, and firmness.

April 1, 1979

She must have planned it for days. Grampie, though he knew he'd been caught every year before, evidently forgot this morning.

Susan appeared early at his window motioning to him as he sat at the kitchen table reading his Bible. "Come quick, Gramp, there's a coon under the front porch."

Grampie obediently tiptoed outside, stooped, and looked under the porch straining to see in the dimness. "I can't see it, Susan," he whispered. "Where is it?"

Behind him, Susan, eyes sparkling and shoulders silently shaking by spells, said, "He's over there, see, in that corner."

Grampie, nearly under the porch by now, still couldn't see it.

Finally she exploded. "April fool!"

Susan and Gramp sat and rocked in laughter together.

May 5, 1979

The air was pure and clear (see II Sam. 23:4) shining after rain this morning. Thin wispy clouds brushed across the blue sky like foam on the sea. It was chilly, but the kind of weather that holds tulips, lilacs, and the new pink fragile leaves in temporary permanence, much better than spring in a three-day heat wave.

Dandelions are blooming thickly. If there were only a few, how we would prize them. Instead, the meadows are a gold carpet and we despise them. Every child loves them and brings bouquets that perish within the hour, the flower that fadeth. Then overnight God turns a field of gold into a thousand cream puffs. Sheer magic this.

Susan took me on a circle tour of all the birds' nests, seven or eight, that she watches daily. The mourning dove in her tidy gray coat had already vacated hers, several blackbirds were noisily presiding over their homes, a tiny sparrow lives in the hemlock hedge with minute babies, and a robin has three exquisite blue eggs in the lilac bush. And high in the maple tree is a Baltimore oriole's abode, a mystery of engineering, hanging precariously over Grampie's driveway.

Now there is that parenthesis of stillness between day and dark when the tulips close their petals as if to pray and the birds sing soft lullabies.

Who could make one day?

June 21, 1979

When I lived in Beirut, one of my dearest friends was Rosalind. She, Margaret, and I lived and taught at the mission school with seven hundred Arab girls, in itself a memorable experience, not to mention all the other things we did, some of which no doubt raised older missionary eyebrows. Once we three crossed the desert on an old bus without air-conditioning, taking three days to reach Baghdad. On the bus was a restroom which was difficult to use as we lurched over the sand (we were not following a road, only the stars, said the driver). So we used it during a stop, only to find out that when we flushed the toilet, everything dropped out in full view of the rest of the tourists. (I wonder, do their airplanes do that also?)

This week Rosalind is *here*, and we are regaling ourselves with stories of those adventurous days. Ed, when he listens, is bemused. Since then, our lives have changed considerably. She is back in London, where she lives with her husband and two children, and I am here in quiet Narvon. Yet how enriched we both are for those years together in the Middle East.

For these three weeks that Ros is here, our days usually begin with a lingering breakfast (scones, eggs, and such with copious amounts of tea), then we go off shopping. Rosalind's favorite is Harry Good's and Kauffman's, both crammed with stuff, bargains and otherwise.

The kids and I took her to Canada for a few days, stopping at Niagara Falls. We stayed in Ontario with the Reeses and Campbells, college mates of mine, a happy reunion.

Rosalind's spirit of joy and praise have been a lift to me in my present physical and mental tiredness at the end of a school year. It is easy to think all Christians must fit into our local pattern, yet God is never bound by culture, custom, nor habit. He has led her in London in a formal church, me in Lancaster County in a free church setting, and we meet the same Christ around a common mercy seat.

Ros's visit has been a lovely reminder of this.

July 5, 1979

It was a rainy, dreary Fourth. Outside and inside. I blew

up when Ed complained about my housecleaning, that I put his things out in the garage and there was no room in the house for his stuff. Why, the house is *full* of his stuff, I exploded. When five people live in a two-bedroom house without even an attic or basement that's usable for storage, something has to give. My stuff, his stuff, the kids' stuff, all has to be sorted each year and thinned out. So I went, on and on.

I slept poorly. (*Let not the sun go down upon your wrath.*) Then I felt exhausted all day. Then he told me of an investment in something which does not seem sensible to me. I seemed to be in a dungeon of dreariness.

How does a wife reconcile what she believes is right with what a husband evidently also believes is right but is the opposite of her instincts? I need to submit; he needs to love. Sometimes just getting it all coordinated, the loving and the submitting, and then practiced (ah, there's the rub) seems more than two can do by themselves.

I guess that's why three are needed in any good marriage. Christ is the only one who can renew love and give a spirit of forgiveness.

July 10, 1979

The sales of the *Guideposts* edition of *Like a Watered Garden* are doing well, and I received a check on Saturday, the largest I've ever received or even seen, modest enough for the likes of Catherine Marshall, I'm sure, but happily surprising to me. Over 150,000 have been sold so far and I can hardly believe such a quiet book could touch so many. *Said I not unto thee that if thou wouldest believe, thou shouldest see the glory of God?* Thus wrote Mrs. McLeod to me when Herald Press first published it. Lord, I believe.

Help thou mine unbelief.

We so desperately need more room that I hoped we could use the royalties as a downpayment on a house, but Ed is not interested. So we remain here.

In the meantime Susan and I, often with wavering faith, go on praying for another little girl and a bigger house.

August 12, 1979

How do people ever get along without children in their home?

Susan is priceless in her remarks, especially when it's an English word she's not sure of. One day she said as she sipped hot tea, "This gives me heartburns."

Then there is Michael, who likes to rescue bugs from the swimming pool and set them safely on the edge. He confided in me one day, "I like to think of the future, Mom, like marriage and heaven and tomorrow." That just about includes it all.

Today they talked Ed into going for my birthday gift and he returned jubilant, having spent their "chicken money" on me. James said he advised Daddy that they shouldn't get me any kitchen stuff, that maybe I got tired of kitchen work and wouldn't like that for my birthday. He has a strong thoughtful streak. He'll make a kind husband someday.

September 6, 1979

In the midst of a cricket-and-katydid concert, with fourteen-day pickles steeping and apple pies simmering, with summer ending and school beginning, with Ruby and Victor returning to Ireland after their visit here—in the middle of all that busyness, Uncle Curtis suddenly left us for that Land which is better, but at seasons like this we sometimes have doubts. I'm sure he did—he loved his quaint whitewashed house and the lovely land around it, the century-old barn, the scent of hay and the taste of Aunt Dee's homemade sauerkraut, his old tractor and the dog following after.

Now he has more, so much more. It's hard to know, to believe how fair heaven is and how much fairer is Jesus' face. I think of the verse from one of Dad's favorite hymns—

> No mortal can with him compare
> Among the sons of men.
> Fairer is he than all the fair
> That fill the heavenly train.

The number there increases, Elizabeth leading the way in 1974. It's becoming more like home all the time.

September 17, 1979

This year Mr. Taylor has moved me back to senior high. I feel in my element again.

I used to tell Ed that my life was a series of trivia from making sandwiches in the morning (who wants mustard? who doesn't like cheese?), all through the day at school (Jane needs help again in long division; Billy's collection of woolly worms *must* go), and into the evening when I must divide the meatballs evenly and help with homework.

Now I can change gears for the several hours that I'm in school. The older students just do not require such detailed care and supervision.

I love teenagers.

October 18, 1979

A funny thing happened on the way to bed. I put the dual-control electric blanket on our bed and went happily to sleep. Waking up too hot, I turned mine down, down, then completely off an hour later. How ever could Ed stand his, I muttered. I kicked off the top blanket. By morning I was baked and had my feet sticking out.

After three nights of this, my quiet Ed complained of being chilly and miserable. "*Chilly?* How in the world . . . you must be sick . . . blah, blah."

Suddenly it came to mind that maybe I had tangled up the cords. When I turned mine off, it was really his. He kept turning his up and I was doing a slow burn.

I began to laugh and he joined me when I was able to explain. I hate to admit it but I think I did the same thing a year ago. Maybe he won't remember that.

October 29, 1979

Tonight, as they often do, Mom and Dad came in about 9:15 for a cup of tea. Then Ed is at work, the children in bed, and I look forward to seeing them, their warm smiles, their eager questions about all of us. They are entirely self-forgetful.

My parents have given me the greatest of gifts, a godly heritage. I thank God daily for them and hope I can pass on even a fraction of that same heritage to my own children.

Tonight Dad told me quietly of a man whom he led to Christ on his Tuesday visitation. In three or four sentences, he tells what most would take paragraphs and pages to say. The overwhelming drive of his life is to tell others about Christ.

Between them, they have probably the most welcoming house in the country. Someone is always stopping by. And anyone who comes receives, if not a meal, at least tea and scone along with the bread of life.

December 10, 1979

The house is beautifully Christmasy. The tablecloth with holly and red cardinals all over it transforms the dining room and reminds me of Rosalind, who has one like it in England. Last summer we bought the material together at Good's and made them. On top of the china cupboard is the log cabin made by my little hunchbacked Uncle George years ago, a miniature of the Russell homestead at the Old Place. Our green tree is shimmering in the living room.

We have everything. Yet in Ireland small cousin Joanne is bedfast now, exceeding ill from the brain tumor and losing her sight while her heartbroken parents watch helplessly. Friend Violet Lewis is having knee surgery in Missouri. In Tehran, the hostages have been kept forty days now with no breakthrough in sight, a sore problem for the president.

But the greatest tragedy of all is the people of Cambodia, especially the children, starving and homeless. The other night I began wrapping gifts in newspaper, then threw down the paper in horror as I saw the photographs of Cambodians, grotesque and dying. What an irony to wrap plastic toys in pictures of dying children. It has haunted me since.

December 24, 1979

Alone by the tree now after a multitude of duties and

celebrations, I feel weariness, but great joy, too. I've had a longing, a deep one, to know Christ in a richer, fuller way this Christmas. He is altogether worthy.

The children opened their gifts tonight, an ecstatic time, and then we had the traditional tea with scone, fruitcake, cookies, cheese, and all such. Tomorrow there will be fifteen here for dinner. The Christmas crowd is diminishing each year, Uncle Curtis spending his first one in heaven. I wonder, do the angels and redeemed celebrate this most awesome night? Does Elizabeth keep Christmas?

God with us. How can it be? The idea is preposterous, incredible, humbling, utterly wonderful. *And she wrapped him . . . Wonderful, Counsellor, the mighty God, The everlasting Father, The Prince of Peace . . . in swaddling clothes, and laid him in a manger.*

January 3, 1980

All evening I've tried to finish a story for *Guideposts*, but first there was supper to get ready and clean up. I enjoy cooking and even dishes are not irksome unless, as tonight, there are just so many other things to do.

There was music practice to guide for all three, and then two games of Authors. I studied science with Susan, perused a map of medieval England with James, looked at the *National Geographic* with both boys, directed baths, read aloud to them from *A Lantern in her Hand,* an old favorite of mine, planned my poetry unit for school, and finally tucked the last one in bed, praying together.

They are so dear and won't be little much longer. Now, at 10:30, I remind myself of that because I was about to be sorry over my unwritten article. Such a story is printed (maybe) and in the glut of today's literature, soon forgotten. These children that I am "writing," forming line upon line, precept upon precept, are stories that have no end. They live forever, and how they live depends largely on Ed and me.

January 10, 1980

Never have I seen anything so exquisite as the hoarfrost feathering every tree and stalk as though a cloud had dusted itself over Pool Forge this morning on the way to school. The sun struck it and with the old covered bridge and the lovely mansion there, it was beyond description.

We stopped the car to look, and I told the children, as I often do, to remember it. We have a near-perfect ride to school each day: our own rustic Narvon Hill, then the Pool Forge Road winding past meadows and farms and creeks, and, finally, Route 23, where we go east through Churchtown, itself a sedate, historic village of handsome old houses, each with a story and various claims to George Washington, who apparently came by every few days and slept a great deal. The brown Bangor Church in the center, one of the oldest in the nation, gives dignity and balance to the village.

Our school is on a ridge overlooking twin valleys that cause visitors to exclaim with delight at the fields like a giant quilt casually thrown down by the generous hand of God.

He hath made everything beautiful in his time, and an extra portion seems to have fallen around us here in Lancaster County.

January 14, 1980

The saga of our cats. A stray turned up a month or two

ago, a pretty gray cat, declawed, obviously a house cat, and completely won Ed's heart. He is extremely susceptible. Because Meatball, also a stray and no doubt insecure, did not take kindly to her, Ed carried the gray one up to the mine to keep him company at work in his little private office. Every day he carried food to her, making special trips on weekends with little jugs of milk and bits and pieces of scraps.

Somehow Smokey, as she came to be named, turned up here again and occupied the basement while Meatball, bedraggled and puny as always, hissed and complained from the front porch. One night Smokey disappeared and Ed kept the basement light on all night, hoping she would return. She did.

Two cats are too much, I said, especially when Meatball is sick all the time. Since it's better to dwell on the housetop than with a contentious woman and since the cat was truly a sight, Ed said he would take Meatball to the vet and do away with her. Susan lay awake last night worrying about that.

Today after school, she rushed inside to hear the details of the cat's demise. Ed was smiling broadly. A kindly old man at the vet's, even more daft about cats than Ed, inquired after her and offered to take her. He had seven other cats but needed one more—to make it even, I suppose. Meatball and the seven drove off in an old 1950 pickup, and Ed, greatly relieved, came home in his old '57 pickup.

January 25, 1980

Today would be Elizabeth's tenth birthday. I wonder, does she ever think of us?

Before supper tonight, I discovered a snowball in James's lunchbox. It was melting all over the table and dampening a box of tissues. Susan, who loves her pranks, had put it there. Just as I was wiping it up with great annoyance and mumblings, she came in the door smiling expectantly, ready to talk as she often does, having quite forgotten her little plot.

I began. "Look at the mess. Don't you see you've ruined the box of tissues? I don't have time for this before supper. If you make a mess, you should clean it up." And so on.

Malicious moralizing.

Suddenly, while setting the table, she burst into tears. "I never do anything right," she wept. I nearly did, too. Susan seldom cries, and I was smitten with guilt. This child, with her self-consciousness, doesn't need me to tear her down, not when she tries so hard to please most of the time. How foolish, how selfish, how vicious it is to hurt a child needlessly.

I had to ask forgiveness, and with a child's generosity, she gave it easily. For Susan I fervently hope the pain will melt as easily as the snowball. But I hope I will not forget to guard my remarks about things that don't matter.

What dear daughters I have.

And that one for whom we pray, Susan and I, will she ever come? Our faith wears thin and we forget and then we remember again.

February 23, 1980

It's been a strange weekend, a strange winter in fact. Ed is in Florida for the second time, looking for a business to buy. To my delight he finally got around to reading my book while there and, better, liked it. "You did a pretty good job, kid," he said. The sweetest compliment I've received.

Tonight, because Ed wasn't here, I took all the kids with me to church. Sometimes they stay home when he's here, and tonight they especially wanted to see Walt Disney's *The Apple Dumpling Gang.*

The preacher, a fill-in since the Palmers moved last month, spoke clearly and with authority. On the way home Susan said quietly, "I'm glad I didn't stay home and see *The Apple Dumpling Gang.*" I hardly noticed her remark.

However, she was no sooner in the house than she grabbed a paper bag, went to the living room, told me to follow her, and shut the door. I was perplexed.

Then with astonishing single-mindedness, she insisted on taking all her Barbie dolls, which had been given to her by other girls, and put them in a bag for Good Will. They *had* to go.

I suggested putting them in Grammie's attic. After all, she had played with them often. But Susan said they must go completely. And even her little cardboard house she and Ed had made must be burned.

"Why, Susan? What brought you to this?"

She said she had been reading the dating column in the paper. (Foolish letters, most of them, with problems that I didn't have till I was twenty, some not then. What are youngsters *doing* today? They're old and jaded before they're ever young.) When Susan read the comics, she would see, and read, the column on the same page.

Her thoughts were often bad, she said, and she knew Jesus was watching her. She hadn't even been able to put up her motto, "I follow Jesus," in her room.

We prayed together. Susan's prayers are always worth

hearing, and I'm sure God thinks so, too. When she hugged me good night, she said as she often does, "I'm so glad I have parents." And she hung up her motto.

For a ten-year-old she has uncommon perception.

If Ed hadn't been in Florida, probably none of this would have happened. And if Elizabeth hadn't gone to heaven six years ago today, Susan would not be here.

Who can know the mind of the Lord?

March 3, 1980

Recently I found this prayer, one of Amy Carmichael's in her book *Kohila*. I read it often and pray it for my children.

> Make them good soldiers of Jesus Christ: let them never turn themselves back in the day of battle.
> Let them be winners and helpers of souls.
> Let them live not to be ministered unto, but to minister.
> Make them loyal; let them set loyalty high above all things.
> Make them doers, not mere talkers; make them sound.
> Let them enjoy hard work and choose hard things rather than easy.
> Forbid that they be slackers. Make them trustworthy. Give them grit.
> Make them wise, for it is written, he hath no pleasure in fools.
> Let them pass from dependence on us to dependence on thee.
> Let them never come under the dominion of earthly things; keep them free.
> Let them grow up healthy, happy, friendly and keen to make others happy.

> Give them eyes to see the beauty of the world and hearts to
> worship its Creator. Cause them to be quick to
> recognize "the figures of the true."
> Let them be gentle to beast and bird; let cruelty be hateful
> to them.
> May they walk, O Lord, in the light of thy countenance. °

March 11, 1980

March, full of wind and promise, must be the ugliest month of the year, rather like a boisterous, ungainly girl of eleven or twelve, who abruptly turns lissome and lovely in another month.

Though we talked again, Ed is still adamant about one thing. He does not want us to buy Mom and Dad's house. It seems logical to me and I long for a bigger house. We are so crowded.

I could persist, insist, get cranky and pesky, but it wouldn't work. Not really. I could "win," but I would lose in the real sense. Manipulating Ed is not what God wants me to do.

Instead, it may be his way of fulfilling another dream, one that I never even uttered as a prayer. It was too impossible. Maybe, maybe, we can use the money, part of it, for all of us to go on a trip to Ireland and England in the summer. That I could see old friends and visit familiar haunts with my dear family hardly bears thinking about.

March 23, 1980

The children are probably at one of their best ages, out of the dependency of early life, and not yet into the self-

---

° *Kohila* (S.P.C.K., 1939), pp. 6-7.

conscious, strident yearning for independence of the teen years.

James is almost afraid to count on the trip. He has so longed to go and has dozens of places we must see, most of them impossible to include. Castles and cathedrals have occupied his mind and reading for some little time now. Presently he's reading all of Thomas Costain's books that he can lay hands on. He is well prepared to go, much better at age eleven than I ever was in my twenties. He asks constantly if I can't just *try* to remember a certain floor plan or details of a cathedral and regretfully I tell him no. Having seen scores of such buildings many years ago, they all roll together in my mind. Friends and people are much clearer.

The only heaviness I feel is that Ed says he won't go. It's enough to dampen my spirit considerably. My persuasiveness has not budged him.

Thus I feel no elation about the prospect of traveling again to the Old World. I know he'll be lonely and dreary here for three weeks. I couldn't bear to be alone that long myself. He shouldn't be left either, no matter how much he says it doesn't matter to him. Why, he might not be here when I got back.

So in spite of James's chatter, I find myself indifferent, praying that God will change Ed's mind. Oh my, having even this bit of money is a burden. Just as well it won't last long.

• • •

Anna in Ireland is gone, the first of the cousins to leave. I remember going to her wedding, my first, when I was thirteen in the little church at Ballymore on our first trip to Ireland.

March 30, 1980

A lovely answer came this evening. After dithering, I chose to stay home from church with the family this evening and, while the children were occupied, I snuggled up to Ed on the couch. He asked about the trip. I told him everything was all right except one grave lack. Then I proceeded to tell him again all the reasons why he should go: that people there were just as nice as here; that he'd see much to interest him; that to be with his family was worth everything and to be absent from them was a pointless loss, one that he might regret later; that he'd gone to Florida alone and now we should go somewhere together—and suddenly he said he'd go. I could have cried and laughed. It was like a burden gone.

When the children found out, Susan said, "Daddy, that's an answer to prayer." It is indeed.

April 23, 1980

Walking around outside this evening, I thanked God audibly for Michael, age nine today.

Such an absent-minded, funny little boy he is. He never even remembered it was his birthday till he got to school and found his desk decorated and a card from his teacher, Kathy Gerhart. His mother was even worse, never remembering till the middle of grocery shopping after school.

An odd thing happened, too. Smokey, our gray cat, was hit by a car and disappeared, likely dead. This made Ed remember our black tomcat that we ran over in our rush to get to the hospital for Michael's birth nine years ago. Mike, who likes cats, seems to be a bit hard on them.

What a beautiful April. Lovely, clear, warm days, the willow tree in the delicate yellow-green stage, periwinkle clambering briskly over the bank in the woods across the road, forsythia in full glory, rhubarb curled tightly waiting to unfurl into pink-striped stalks. As I walked, it reminded me of Michael's budding potential and that's when I thanked God for him.

He was the third baby in twenty-seven months. I remember the exhaustion. But what if we hadn't had him?

May 24, 1980

Mom has come through her mastectomy exceptionally well. Many have prayed. I saw her today and she looks bright, rested, and without pain. Ed gave blood for her. That touched her. I was rejected. "Too low in iron," they said, so I'll have to eat lots of our spinach.

She must have radium treatments for twenty-three days. That will pretty well occupy the next three weeks for Dad, getting her to Lancaster each day. And so, for another year their trip to Ireland has had to be postponed.

Yet Mom's health, never strong, has a surprising resilience, and she has a certain stubborn tenacity that gives her more endurance than I'll ever have.

June 14, 1980

In reading Elizabeth Goudge's book *Pilgrim Inn*, I am moved to pray more intently than ever that God would give us one day a big house to make it a refuge for our family and for many others as well in years to come. My parents' home has been like a city, a light set on a hill that cannot be hid, and people have come from afar for physical and spiritual nourishment that Mom and Dad have given generously all these many years. Their guests must number in the thousands and scarcely a one has not sat down for tea, along with the living bread. Those who eat it shall live forever. They have given that bread to so many.

God knows my longing.

July 4, 1980

The Fourth of July is a watershed, the dividing line of summer. Before it, the season looks limitless; afterward, it seems to go downhill.

The kids cut the grass, Mike managing to get stung twice. I scurried around cleaning and cooking.

A picnic of ham, various salads, fruit, and desserts here at our picnic table that Ed built. Russell's family, Mom and Dad, Aunt Ruth, all joined us for dinner. Later McConaghays stopped by and also Betty Ann, helping us eat the leftovers for supper. We played baseball, lit sparklers, all under one of those skies whose clarity makes one ache for—what? That Land beyond the sky where, though now we see through a glass, darkly, we shall see clearly one day.

I am peacefully thrilled about our trip that begins on Monday. It is vast relief to know Ed will go. The children and I are leaving a week before him, thus requiring him to miss less work, and I will get some of my womanly visiting done with Rosalind, with whom we'll stay in London. He will join us for a few days in London. Then we'll go to Ireland for ten more days. It sounds unbelievable and absolutely marvelous. All praise to the God of dreams.

The kids, in pajamas, are outside studying the stars now. I pray that they will always love high things, things which, as Paul says, are true and honest, just and pure and lovely and of good report.

July 11, 1980—Dorset, England

For three days we are making our home in a manor house that once belonged to Henry VIII and Catherine Parr, his sixth wife and the only one who managed to survive him. Now it's the home of my cousin Audrey and her family, all of whom I had never met till this trip because they lived and worked for years in the Caribbean with Barclay's Bank.

She has truly welcomed us into this lovely estate, their place of retirement. The house has enormous rooms. My favorite is the main hall or dining room with its fireplace, window seats, long table, and a wide staircase salvaged from an old ship leading to the second floor. I can imagine the magic of this room at Christmas. Aunt Nell lives upstairs in a large comfortable room, looking frail but cheerful.

Out front is a pre-Christian tomb, used now for a colorful flower box! We have walked under the immensely spreading, centuries-old trees, to see Don's gardens where grow the healthiest gooseberries and black currants I've ever seen. What a beautiful place. I wish Ed were here.

The boys and I walked about the village yesterday in the long English twilight, looking into the exquisite gardens of cottages with names like The Bees and Primrose Cottage. Some were behind walls and we stood peering in at the gate trying to glimpse a bit. There is something so tantalizing about a walled garden.

Audrey is taking us to some local cathedrals, castles, and we drove through Sturminster, the setting for some of Thomas Hardy's novels.

James, after a severe case of jet lag, is in ecstasy to see what he has read about for so long.

July 13, 1980—London

We took a memorable weekend trip to Cambridge, Ely Cathedral, and Bury St. Edmonds, where Rosalind's sister Ruth lives. What names these British have! Then we drove home by way of Lavenham in Suffolk.

It was a sentimental stop for me, one that I wanted the children to make. It was fourteen years ago that I had stayed there in the rectory, Ros's home then. With idle time on my hands, I had written a story about the final Billy Graham meeting at Wembley Stadium. Months later in November 1966, that story was published in *Decision*. Ed Read wrote to me. Our courtship went from there, by mail for several months, and at last face-to-face.

So without this charming little village of Lavenham, they, the children, would quite literally not be here. And without the book, whose first chapter contained the story of our romance and whose profits we are using, we would not be touring this sceptered isle. It was a singular delight to walk along streets where I had once walked as an exceedingly lonely single person, wondering if God would ever give me a husband and family. How could I have known or even guessed then what God must have smiled to know?

There are incredibly crooked timbered houses in Lavenham, one which, in fact, inspired the nursery rhyme about the crooked man who lived in a crooked house. James and I even sneaked into the beautiful, haughty Swan Hotel to see the elegant Tudor rooms.

We had a delicious cream tea in a tiny crowded tearoom. Then we drove back to London in a horrendous traffic jam, getting miserably lost. Rob stayed home, probably to preserve his sanity. He let me drive his car all weekend, a feat of faith on his part, I'm sure.

July 15, 1980

Rosalind, always a resourceful woman, came up with an inspired idea this morning, the only day yet that began with sunshine. It was the Queen Mother's 80th birthday, and in honor of the occasion there was to be a procession to St. Paul's.

Ros gathered us up right after breakfast and led us to Fleet Street where, being early, we had an ideal place to stand and could nearly touch the passing cars and carriages.

First came notables in Rolls Royces, dressed in high style, moving slowly, since it was near St. Paul's, their destination. We had time to gawk at them. One we knew, Margaret Thatcher, who looked directly at us and smiled at our crowd of eager children, my three and Mark and Fiona.

What splendid pageantry these English have! The horses, scores of them in gleaming harnesses, their riders in red uniforms, and finally, what we'd waited for, the members of the royal family in open carriages. There were Princess Anne and her husband, Princess Margaret, Queen Elizabeth and Prince Philip, and at last, the Queen Mother, gracious in a lavender hat, sitting with her favorite, Prince Charles.

Before the trip, Susan had said the one thing she wanted to see was the queen. "Oh, darling," I said, "I've been to England many times and I've never seen the queen. That just won't happen."

I should never have said that. God hears the prayers of children, and Susan's dream came true.

July 16, 1980—London

Today I had another touch with my past, a lovely link,

and a faint picture of what heaven will be. Rosalind, who has taken a great deal of trouble for us, planned to have six of the dear missionary women we had known from our Beirut days here for lunch.

I had the responsibility of picking up Iris Naish. But I got muddled up and went to the wrong side of the train station. Till I maneuvered around the streets to the other side, Iris was nowhere in sight. Susan and I pursued her and found her striding along with her handbag and satchel of goodies for the children as purposefully as ever she strode over the Lebanese mountains in her beloved village work. Intrepid soul, one of Britain's finest.

She, with Pauline and Lottie, are now retired, but still vibrantly interested in Lebanon and the trials there and in us; they are still growing. Their sturdy faith that I knew when I was too young and inexperienced to appreciate fully, has not declined nor grown dim, but rather increased.

As happens more often now, I was meeting with a group that would probably never again all be together here, but There we will and then with Another as well.

● ● ●

This evening the five children and I went by underground into Oxford Street to the Palladium, where *The King and I* is playing, starring Yul Bryner. Susan and James loved it. Susan was especially fascinated by the adorable Oriental children in the play. The other three squirmed their way through, causing great ire in the man behind us.

Ed is probably boarding about now to fly over. I'll meet him, joyfully, in the morning at Heathrow.

July 21, 1980—Dublin

Regretfully, we left Rosalind and her children this morning. Rob took us to Euston Station, a thoughtful boost on his way to work. That eased the suitcase problem. Ed carries the big ones; I knew I needed him on this trip. He has truly enjoyed England, a surprise to himself and a joyful relief to me.

We boarded an amazingly fast train that rushed us across England and Wales in a matter of hours. I've never on the ground traveled so swiftly.

At Holyhead we boarded the *St. Columba,* traveling across the Irish Sea to Dublin. It was an idyllic day, the first one of complete sunshine. We watched the gulls swooping and wheeling and the wake swirling behind the ship. We bought snacks, explored the ship, and thoroughly enjoyed being a family alone all day. It was both exhilarating and relaxing.

In Dublin we saw Cecil, peering into the crowd searching for us. He and Betty welcomed us to an ample supper and overnight lodging before we travel north tomorrow to Donegal in a rented car.

July 23, 1980—Galdonagh, Donegal

I can't think of any house that is easier to settle into than here with Uncle Thomas and Aunt Katy. All five of us roared up the lane yesterday thinking we would have a dramatic entrance. We found, instead, that the man whose car we had followed briefly was a neighbor who rushed ahead and announced our imminent arrival. It brought to mind the time, years ago, when I grandly came from St. Johnston in a taxi. The driver, none too careful, bumped the bicycle of a small boy, tumbling him into the ditch.

With large frightened eyes, he assured us he was all right. Then, like a jackrabbit, he scuttled across the meadow. When the taxi pulled up at the house, minutes later, the whole family awaited me—along with the small boy who was my cousin Bobby. It is hard for Yankees to arrive quietly.

Uncle Thomas is like Dad with gentle humor and crinkly eyes, enormous hands and easygoing manner. In recent years constant arthritic pain has gradually brought to a halt the ceaseless labor he enjoyed. The children like to watch and help him with the milking.

Aunt Katy, herself an orphan as a child, has always mothered anyone who ever turned up. All morning one or several are eating continuously at the table while she makes fresh pots of tea and gets dinner ready.

The table stretches. Sometimes only five or six, more often as now, ten or twelve sit down at noon to Irish sausages and "mince" or a couple of chickens, along with a big pot of potatoes. I think of Granny, how she used to take a new potato from the pot, peel the skin, dip it in salt, and contentedly eat by the fire.

We had hardly arrived till the family began to troop in: eight children, greatly increased now through marriage, and a whole new set of small cousins to meet. Beautiful, apple-cheeked towheads, most of them.

July 25, 1980—Galdonagh

When I visited Ireland in 1974 soon after Elizabeth's death, we sang hymns together at Aunt Rebecca's house. Sue, her daughter, and always a favorite cousin of mine, hugged me and said, "Maureen, how can you sing?"

Months later, we heard that Sue's little daughter,

79

Joanne, had a brain tumor. I wrote Sue and said maybe God was teaching her to sing, too.

Joanne lived on for several years until last spring, her parents watching the gradual dissolution of her health. Sue, a nurse, tenderly cared for her at home until the last dark night in April when it ended.

Today we went to Derry to see Sue and Ronnie, talking at length and visiting the grave, with memories of our own little grave far away. As I watched Sue, there was a clear reminder of the grace of God in times of either sudden or slow death. He gives songs in the night.

• • •

It is well that I assured myself of Aunt Katy's big heart, for it must be stretched to the limit tonight.

Earlier, before we ever left the States, I had written Mary Rogers Smith, with whom I had had marvelous adventures in Cairo, in Jerusalem, in Aquaba, as well as hilarious times at the girls' school in Beirut. Mary was the one who, in true Scots' fashion, had taught me to bargain in the *souks* of the Middle East. Since then, she had married, and turning out to be even more fertile than I, was the mother of four children.

"Mary, find a way to leave your family, fly to London, and meet me there for a few days," I urged.

But Mary, her own person as always, decided that was a wee bit frivolous. It would be better, she reasoned, to go by boat to Ireland with her two sons along, the girls being on holiday elsewhere, since three could travel by boat-train for the price of one by air. Besides, Ireland appealed to her more.

Thus it was that Mary came to Derry, where we met her today with her two sons. Eight people stuffed into our small English car made a crowded ride. The house was tumultuous, what with all of Aunt Katy's family in and out as well.

When I sent the kids to bed, Uncle Thomas said, "That's the best news I heard yet."

July 26, 1980—Galdonagh

The rain is impossible, "the wettest summer in three hundred years," says a local wag. Certainly it is worse than any I've seen, and I so wanted good weather this year for the family, especially Ed. I want him to *like* Ireland. Weather can affect one's opinions forever, really.

Anne Hay Thompson took us, Mary's family and ours, to Marble Hill Strand this afternoon. It rained the whole wretched time, though beautifully too, in a misty, Irish way. The Strand is a lovely white beach cove with green hills round about, invisible today because they were covered in mist.

We meant to picnic at Ards but instead piled in at Aunt Annie Jane's, her quaint, low-raftered house being a kind of hub in Creeslough around which relatives and friends revolve. Pink-cheeked and good-natured as always, she was quite bemused as we, a total of thirteen big and little folk, occupied her neat kitchen. The children steamed in their wet clothes by the fire, and the mothers passed out tea and sandwiches to everyone. Ed and Aunt Annie chatted like old friends. There was a grand racket.

In the middle of it, Uncle John and Aunt Grace turned up, watching in amazement till we left, then no doubt commiserating with Aunt Annie on the strange ways of

American tourists. Being kind, tolerant people, they probably had a good laugh.

Anne, bless her, invited us, for the second time this week, to tea, which is quite an elegant supper at her place. She lives in an old town house on the Diamond in Raphoe.

July 27, 1980

Prayer is such a powerful, inexplicable thing. It reaches from Narvon to this little place called Creeslough and then up to heaven, a wonderful triangle of love and intercession.

We attended church here on the old homeplace at Rooskey, where Dad and all the eleven children grew up, now occupied by my cousin Bob and his family. Bob and Jean, ardent believers, have a tiny hall where a small group meets weekly.

As I sat there this morning, I remembered all the prayers, spoken and silent, Dad prayed for Ireland and for his family over the years. This little church is a kind of symbol of those prayers and of what God is doing in Ireland today.

It was a family day, the kind I love. After a superb dinner, we visited Aunt Rebecca and her family, including a clutch of small grandsons. She has a warm heart and gave us tea in her home with homemade muffins and delectable black currant jam that I remember from my childhood.

Then to Roscad to my gallant Uncle George, whom I have never seen anything but cheerful and praising God. Physically handicapped, he has never submitted to any physical or spiritual limitations.

From there we went to Doe Castle, an isolated spot, and browsed among the ruins. The castle, on a point of land jutting into an inlet of the sea, is a paradise for a child like

James who loves the mystery and beauty of medieval times. The youngsters clambered over walls, climbed the tower, stood in the immense fireplace, toured the cemetery, and ate wild gooseberries.

July 30, 1980—Galway

Good-byes are always wrenching. One is never sure, especially as folks grow older, if it is the last farewell.

So it was today, as we said good-bye to these dear ones. In our rented car we drove down the narrow lane at Galdonagh for the last time, looking back and waving, then headed south. Stopping in Donegal town, we bought fruit to eat along the way, gasping over the price.

What a beautiful day, perhaps our best. The Yeats country in the golden light with cloud shadows scudding across Ben Bulben was especially lovely. Along the coast we traveled, into Galway, stopping this evening at a bed-and-breakfast home of one, Bridie McKee, who with her family made us most welcome. For the price of an average motel, we not only have a place to sleep, but in the morning we'll have an abundant Irish breakfast of sausages, bacon, eggs, two or three kinds of bread and scones, and gallons of tea.

We're just an hour or more from Shannon Airport. Tomorrow night we'll sleep at Narvon and our dream trip will be a memory.

Bless the Lord, O my soul, and forget not all his benefits.

August 10, 1980

Though we regretfully came back from Ireland, part of it has followed us. The day after our arrival, Bob and Jean Hay flew in to New York also and have stayed with Mom and Dad across the road. The teapot is always on the stove. Exactly one week after we had Sunday dinner with them, they ate with us.

Today our new pastor, Argyl Dick, and his family were at church for his first Sunday. He is a loving man, warm, interested in people, and seems to be balanced in his preaching. There are always rumblings and adjustments to a new pastor, but this man seems truly humble, which should go a long way toward easing tensions.

After eight months without a pastor, there is a kind of relief, a sense of purpose again at church.

August 11, 1980

Russell has begun in the past summer or two to buy inexpensive old houses, repair, paint, restore, and then rent them. This year he got one in Lebanon, Pennsylvania, where I went today to help him paper and paint. Unfailingly good-natured, original in his opinions, with a self-mocking and somehow touching sense of humor, he is fun to work with. I love him dearly.

We talk about everything, Russ and I; politics (his first love), school, writing, kids, faith. A local tragedy has eclipsed all news for the present. Andy and Ruth Fisher, members of our church, discovered their fourteen-year-old daughter, Evie, was missing on the 31st, the day we flew home from Ireland. It is now the twelfth day and she has not been found. We have all ached for them.

August 15, 1980

Ed suffers often from sleeplessness, something I've pondered much over the years. Last night we prayed together as a family and I read aloud from Ephesians 6. How vulnerable our minds are. We need that armor of God described so clearly there.

And tonight he and I read those beautiful verses in Psalm 4 about sleep, the final one, "I will both lay me down in peace, and sleep: for thou, Lord, only makest me dwell in safety." We prayed again, a sweet time.

This morning early, I had a dream about him—he was so happy and very tender—and I've prayed for him all day.

• • •

Susan recently said to me again, "Mom, will we ever have another girl?" And I answered, "Go and ask Daddy once more."

Now Ed has this wonderful way of avoiding an answer. He holds his newspaper a little higher and concentrates mightily.

Susan came back discouraged. "He won't answer, Mom."

What can I say more than I have already? If God wills, she'll come to us. If it is not God's plan we cannot insist. It's a lesson in submission for Susan and me, both to an earthly father and the heavenly Father.

September 4, 1980

The reading from *Daily Light* this morning was this: "Sit still, my daughter. Take heed and be quiet; fear not, neither be fainthearted. Be still and know that I am God. Said I not unto thee, that if thou wouldest believe, thou shouldest see the glory of God?"

It was a singularly appropriate word for my first day *ever* to have specific time set aside to write. This year I asked Mr. Taylor if he would let me teach just three days a week, spending Tuesday and Thursday at home. His wife, Sue, with whom I work well, will be my co-teacher. This system, I hope, will work in the ACE program, at least for senior high. I have had such a yearning to write and no time to indulge it.

Sitting here by the window this morning, I am full of excitement and anticipation, yet I'm also timid and a bit fainthearted. What if I can't produce? (The neighbor's bantam rooster is happily crowing on his way up to our harem of chickens in the woods. No faintheart he!)

And yet, if I believe, I shall see the glory of God. The *glory* of God.

So I begin, first to sort through my heaps of papers and files, and then to choose what to write.

September 16, 1980

For a long time I have been bothered by an emphasis in Christian writing. All the books about people are of religious or political leaders, or those who have achieved fame by experiencing something dramatic, sudden wealth or health, survival of an accident, release from a gross sin, whatever.

But what of us ordinary folk living lives that may be placid, dreary, colorless? Can Christ give meaning and worth and richness to such? He most certainly can and does. I have wanted to see a book that illustrates this—the story of a man or woman who lives a quiet life, yet whose faith outlines every ordinary day with glory, whose life is merely an earthen vessel but with that treasure which is Christ.

In thinking on this, it came to me rather suddenly that I should write about Dad. Beginning on a farm in Ireland, his is an interesting life yet not at all sensational. He worked in a factory most of his adult life, doing hard labor, yet everyone he met was touched by the presence of Christ. And still they are. He is a living believable man who has chosen to follow the Lord wholly.

So I have begun my book of an ordinary man who lives an extraordinary life of faith. It may be only for our children's eyes, for it is not the kind of story that will grab a publisher. Books must sell, make money, and this one might not. A writer's dreams do not always produce hard cash.

But then, there is always the chance that one editor will find an appeal in it for the common person. All I need is one.

October 9, 1980

At last the truth is known, dreadful as it is. Evie Fisher's body was found ten weeks almost to the hour after she disappeared. This morning a local policeman, Rod Hartman, found her in a heavily wooded part of the Welsh Mountain, an area where even her own father had searched and called for her in the days following her disappearance. The massive search is now over and we know she is gone.

Though it was what we all expected, the news shattered me when I heard it. I can imagine how her parents feel after the excessive emotional strain they've been under.

She was brutally murdered, only God and one other know how brutally, and the trial can now proceed in the leisurely way such events happen with much posturing and planning by lawyers, hearings, delays, and what not.

Evie was to have been one of my students at school this year. Now she knows far more than I could ever teach her.

October 12, 1980

Susan spent her first five years at An Lac Orphanage in Saigon before she came to us. Recently on television there was a documentary film, showing how Betty Tisdale and Ina Balin evacuated these children in April 1975. Those over ten had to be left behind. It was a heart-wrenching scene as the little ones board the buses for the airport while the older ones stood with Madame Ngai and watched forlornly.

Little Vu Thi Dinh, now Susan Read, was one who flew out. We all wept furtively and silently, remembering her arrival and what that has meant to us.

October 25, 1980

God knew what he was doing when he invented grand-mothers. There was my mother in her "sewing room," piled high with junk. Mom is an irrepressible collector.

And there was my son Michael with her, both of them burrowing in boxes and bags and heaps, both talking contentedly. I felt like an intruder.

Michael came home later with a complete outfit for Halloween, some books to read, old photos to show me, a quaint basket with a screw-top lid, and a satisfied smile. It had been a good afternoon.

"Mommy, Grammie sure has a lot of nice stuff," he said appreciatively. "And she likes me to look at it with her."

Grandmothers are like that. They have plenty of old things and plenty of time. And they like little boys (and girls) to look and talk with them. In a busy, tightly scheduled world, it is a wonderfully reassuring security for a small child to have a grammie who is warm and loving and *slow*.

December 28, 1980

George Seldomridge, probably 80 or more, has been on my mind and in my prayers for a long time. He and Anna are such good neighbors, but I've wondered often if George truly knows Christ, whom to know is life eternal.

This afternoon I stopped in and visited a bit, then asked them trembling, if they had Jesus in their hearts. Anna said yes, but George said he wasn't baptized.

"That wasn't what I asked," I said, "but rather, Do you know Christ?" He said he hoped so.

I told him that one accepts him by faith, and the Word of God promises us that we can then *know* he is ours forever. *These things have I written unto you that believe on the name of the Son of God; that ye may know that ye have eternal life. . . .*

I told him how, years ago, I had come to Christ as a small child. Baptism, church membership, giving money, none of these were enough. Only the blood of Jesus could wash our sins away. I told him about the thief on the cross, that all he could do was give his sin to Jesus. There was no time to be baptized, yet Jesus said they would be *today* together in paradise.

George's eyes were wet. He said I was only the second person that ever told him salvation is a gift from God, that it hinges only on what Christ did.

Now I'm praying that the Spirit of God will make it clear to George.

January 9, 1981

James was twelve on January 6. It is hard to believe that the little scrap I brought home from the hospital my firstborn, is now verging on his teens. I think of all the sleepless hours, the hard work, the utter weariness invested just in this one son, and, in a faint picture of how God felt, I see that it is good. A child is an investment in the future and I pray that James will bless many.

He is a dear son, sensitive and conscientious, probably too much so for his own peace of mind. All his life he will be prodded by some inner goad to try harder, to reach toward perfection. In school he reminds his teacher when he has an assignment due. There are no shortcuts for James.

• • •

In my prayers for our children, I pray for those other children who will one day marry ours. I timidly mention that James will need a wife who will listen when he talks about his dreams and when he worries about things; that Susan ought to have a husband who will enjoy her athletic abilities; that she really would like someone who looks like her; that it would be pleasant indeed if they could marry someone not too far away; that Mike with his touch of whimsy should have an understanding wife when he forgets to empty the garbage.

These are really small things. The real prayer, the one that matters, is for them to have homes that are loving and godly, *that the generation to come . . . even the children who should be born . . . might set their hope in God . . . and keep his commandments.*

The greatest contribution one can make to the church or to the nation is a stable home, a family where honesty, kindness, and integrity are taught, where the Word of God is honored. This is what I desire most for my children and their future homes.

90

January 17, 1981

One of my most admired people is Amy Carmichael, though I've never met her and never can till we meet in that better world.

An Irish woman, she gave her life in India to the care of children, little girls (later boys as well) whom she rescued from a life of temple prostitution.

Recently another of her books has come to my attention. All of them are profound; none were ever bestsellers. They cannot be read in a hurry.

Let me write here what is sheer poetry, what says in words my best innermost longings:

> My flesh and my heart faileth—let them fail. For God is the strength of my heart and my portion for ever. Has anyone ever been able to tell what our glorious Lord can be to man, woman, or little child whom He is training to wait upon Him only?
>
> No one has ever been able to tell it. I search for words like jewels, or stars, or flowers, but I cannot find them. I wish I could, for this book may fall into the hands of someone who has been hindered from caring to know Him by the dull and formal trapping which our dull and formal thoughts have laid upon Him—strange disguise for such a radiance. How can I commend my Master? I have not seen Him yet, but I have caught glimpses. . . .
>
> Without Him, Lover of all lovers, life is dust. With Him it is like the rivers that run among the hills, fulfilled with perpetual surprises. He who knows his Lord as Saviour and King is taken, as old Richard Rolle declares, into a marvelous mirth, so that he as it were sings his prayers without notes. Life is battle—yes, but it is music. It knows the thrill of brave music, the depths and heights of music. It is *life,*

not stagnation. Oh, taste and see that the Lord is good. Blessed (happy, very happy) is the man that trusteth in Him.°

January 26, 1981

Ed and I are again haggling over finances. Months slide by and we have only minor scrapes, then something jars everything loose that we've carefully built up. Marriage is rather like our swallow's nest under the eaves that can withstand wind and storm, but a thoughtless bump can shake it loose. We, like the small birds, flit here and there, putting the pieces together again.

I don't know how anyone manages without God to lean on and a solid, unshakable belief that marriage is forever. It's the only way to keep it, and it *is* worth keeping.

February 26, 1981

Tonight Mom is in the hospital, nearly unconscious with a raging fever, over 104 much of the time. It began Tuesday night when, very tired, she lay on the couch to rest, something she often does. Dad, who had been out all day visiting for the church, urged her to come to bed soon. Then he went himself, knowing she would follow in her own good time. Mom was never one to follow a schedule.

However, early in the morning he woke and found her still on the couch, incoherent by spells, utterly miserable. The doctor thought it could be a severe flu, but when she continued so ill, we called the ambulance.

As it drove off with her this morning, I felt a great heartache. Her illness began the day after Elizabeth's

---

°*Gold Cord* (S.P.C.K., 1952), pp. 62-63.

death-day and I remembered the high fever and horror of that time, her leave-taking, never to return again.

She seemed to rally a bit when the ambulance came, but then Mom has an incredible drive to respond to people, to put her best foot forward, to smile. Later, in the hospital, she was as sick as ever. At least she has an IV to keep her from completely dehydrating.

Dad stopped in late tonight, and as I gave him a cup of tea, we wondered if we should have stayed all night with her.

Will she ever come back? No one seems to know the cause, so they can't treat it. I wept while mailing letters— no lights at home where she always is.

March 1, 1981

When he got to the hospital yesterday morning, Dad called me and said Mom was worse. She didn't smile and every breath continued to be a little gasping moan. Her body was swollen and to touch her hurt her.

"Her kidneys aren't working right," he said. And I remembered. My Grandmother Russell had died that way.

Leaving the kids with Ed in a little huddle of heartache, I rushed in. When I saw her I fully expected it to be my last hours with her. She seemed scarcely to know me, though Russell, when he came, received a brief, sweet smile.

She was in such misery that I prayed for a quick release. Her moaning, gagging, the utter distortion of her features made death seem a friend.

Nurses came and went, prodding, turning, taking blood, seeming only to torment her further. At last a specialist turned up who suggested it was a severe blood infection. Dad, who was himself wracked by misery, feared that to do anything now would only compound her wretchedness. He wanted no experiments, no more painful tests.

"Penicillin," insisted the doctor, "just might do it."

It seemed too easy but was worth a try. And with nearly the first drip into her arm, she seemed to rally, slowly, slowly, but ever so surely. We were watching a miracle take place right in front of us.

Russ and I stayed all night, but the tide had turned. She was mending. We have Mom a little longer.

March 5, 1981

Eight inches of snow kept us home both from school and the hospital. I cleaned Mom's bedroom.

She is still improving steadily, seeming more herself all the time. It will take months for a full recovery, and so for the third time their trip to Ireland will be canceled.

With her illness, my momentum has been broken in writing my story about Dad, his family, his life. At times I lose faith in it completely. Then when I reread bits, it sounds good. It is hard to evaluate one's own writing, rather like judging your own children. Some things you know are good about them, but it's hard to see easily what are flaws, and harder still to correct them.

March 15, 1981

One day in school Pastor Dick with his guileless smile said to me, "You know what happened, don't you, as a result of your Jim Smith story in January *Guideposts*?"

I smiled and said I thought Jim had probably sold some stoves because of it, and I was praying that people who read it would be touched spiritually in some way.

He smiled more broadly, if that's possible. "A man

received Christ because of it."

I could hardly believe what I was hearing. Why, the story had been a bit drab, as *Guideposts* stories go, not at all dramatic. A man converted? Through that little workaday article?

Then I remembered. God has chosen the foolish things to confound the wise. He takes what is in our hand, a shepherd's staff, a loaf of bread, a pen, and multiplies it with his touch to bless many.

The following Sunday the man, Otto Schumann, was in church. At the end of the service during the invitation, he walked forward in his dignified, gray, pin-striped suit and publicly acknowledged his allegiance to Christ.

Lately I've been discouraged with writing. Nothing has sold, and it seemed as though it was all in vain, that maybe I am chasing rainbows.

Today, a week later, I met Otto, a warm, rejoicing man, who thanked me for the story. And I remembered again how God fulfills dreams, prayers, and sometimes even rainbows. *Not unto us, O Lord, not unto us, but unto thy name give glory.*

Hope

---

*Happy is he [she] whose hope is in the
Lord . . . .*

At last, at last, after all the years of thinking and praying,
plans were progressing for another child to come to us. We
could hardly wait to see her. Why did it take so long? I
cherished a small photo, looking at it often.

And there are times also when I can hardly wait to see
Jesus, the one I've loved increasingly over the years, the
one who has given me life and breath and all the joys I
have. When will we see him? What is heaven really like?

Our little Korean daughter, so far away, whom we had
never seen, was an illustration of the hope every Christian
has to see and know him face-to-face.

Come with me and follow our hearts as we wait and
pray, doubt and trust, fear and hope.

Chapter

2

March 21, 1981

I was lying peacefully on the couch this afternoon trying to catch a snooze, as is my habit in odd moments, when Ed nonchalantly showed us a photo of an Oriental child in the *Inquirer.* Called "Friday's Child," she was older and needed a home. Susan was entranced.

Rather sharply, I said, "Why show us that, Ed, if we can't do anything about it? You're just tantalizing us."

Without argument, he simply said, "Phone if you like and inquire about her." Perhaps he *hadn't* been so indifferent all these years.

I nearly leaped off the couch, lest he change his mind, and began phoning. The agency was, of course, closed on a Saturday afternoon.

But the step is made. I've never known Ed to back down once he's made a step forward. He's a man of his word.

The first prayer began for "two little girls" before Susan came. Then she and I prayed for "another girl and a bigger house." Is this the beginning of the answer? We were already discussing names, a class in school, clothes, and such.

It is the beginning of spring. And Mom is home. Today was the first Saturday in three months that I haven't visited the sick, first Betty Ann, who became ill on New Year's Eve, and this last month Mom in the hospital. I baked all morning and loved it. God is good.

April 16, 1981

Is there anything so *hopeful* as April? Today is brilliant after a long, steady, wonderful rain. Tulips nod outside the kitchen window, the pear tree looks like old lace against the blue sky, and wild geese honk imperiously morning and evening. Some have taken up residence behind us around the old mine hole.

For my Good News Club today after school, I had made some pita bread, similar to that found in the Middle East. I broke it and passed it out to the children. *This do in remembrance of me.* The enormity of his sacrifice struck me and I wanted to weep telling them about it.

We've asked for the Korean girl, aged 12, and when I phoned about her today, they said we are first under consideration. *Praying always ... and watching thereunto...."*

Watching, watching hard for her arrival.

May 22, 1981

Can it be? She *is* to come to us, the child for whom we applied over two months ago, then thought we were rejected. The agency simply would not answer our letters of inquiry and phone calls were vague, never the right person when we called. Tonight I phoned again, Susan begging me, this time to our own local agency, Tressler-Lutheran in York. Barb said they themselves were getting no answers till just lately, that the agency had had a tragic result with one of their placements, and were now checking applicants more thoroughly than ever.

However, they have weighed us in the balance and evidently have not found us wanting, for she said *we are approved.*

My mind spins with ideas. Will we possibly get her this summer? That would give us a pillow of adjustment before school. Where will we sleep? My tandem prayer, another girl and a bigger house, are not necessarily answered together. She must be planned for somewhere in this present two-bedroom house; that takes thought. What grade will she fit into? She'll have English to learn. Will she and Susan want to share clothes? We're advised to change her name—will she like *Anne?*

Just as well I'm so excited, since the query on my Irish story was returned, rejected, today. The manuscript is not complete yet by any means, but I wanted to send out a feeler. Should I even bother to finish? Is there worth in it? I acknowledge readily it needs much polishing, but I had hoped the theme and the tone of it would find a sympathetic editor, one who would recognize the treasure in the earthen vessel.

I cannot stop. Quitters never get published.

June 1, 1981

Graduation. Ten young people on the edge of adulthood, taking that step of independence from which there is no return.

As I consider it, there is probably nothing I would enjoy more than what I do right now, teaching in a Christian school. It is satisfying to invest time, energy, creativity, patience in people, people who will live forever, who were created in God's image, who can respond and laugh and grow and learn. I love teenagers, their crazy sense of humor, their moods, their wonderful idealism, their unpretentiousness.

Tonight there were speeches, testimonies, diplomas, smiles, tears, love, and thanksgiving, all focusing on the goodness of God, making the weary days, the crowded hours, the small paychecks all worthwhile.

June 3, 1981

I seem to be thrust into confusion and a kind of depression, heavier than usual. Some domestic tension here at home, but more than that, a perplexing problem about our "other" child.

A packet about her came from Tressler. It turns out she has a mother with whom she lives along with five brothers and sisters. I was shocked. Never do I want to break up a family. What had happened?

In phoning Barb, I found that this is fairly common. A Korean parent or family decides to send a child to America, giving up all rights, so the child can have a better life. It is obviously done out of love, so the child will be educated and have all the advantages of America.

But for me, I cannot *think* of taking a girl from her family. Why, every night I would wonder about that bereft mother and what she was thinking. Was she crying? Did she long to put her arms around her once more? Somehow my experience with Elizabeth—the ache to see her, touch her just one more time—gives me a sense of horror about it which I can't convey even to Ed.

I told Barb I wanted a daughter who had no love, no

family, a truly impoverished child. One who has a loving mother and even simple food is not really deprived as some are.

She suggested another, younger girl, a six-year-old, but Ed is not easy about that. It will mean changing gears and thinking small again now that our other three are older.

On top of all that is the expense, a huge amount of money.

I need to pray, and I'm so tired. Ed is at work and there's no one to talk to.

June 4, 1981

Last night in my low estate, as David puts it, I phoned Jackie to get some information about a story I'm doing on her for *Power*. She assured me of her prayers for our girl, and I went to bed easier. I woke to sunshine and a much lighter heart, for which I couldn't account till later in the day when I remembered Jackie's promise to pray. God had heard and lifted me considerably.

This morning, once more, I explained my feelings to Ed, that for me it would be wrong to take a child from a family where she was loved. I just plain could not do it, though I'm sorry, since this was the girl he had particularly wanted. Seeing my agitation and thinking through the problem, he agreed that we should instead take the six-year-old, unless her age prohibits this. We *are* old to be starting again with a first-grader.

I phoned Barb about our decision, and we all felt better afterward. Actually, for Susan, a small one might be easier, less rivalry for her who has always been the apple of Ed's eye.

A final irony: just a couple days ago, Susan and I, in a

spasm of housecleaning and trying to make more room, gathered up the box of little girl's clothes we'd hoarded, in faith, ever since Susan herself had worn them and hauled them off to Good Will thinking we were getting the twelve-year-old. Now they are just what we need and they're gone.

June 12, 1981

The years rolled away and it all came back to me: the good-natured crowd, the music, the sunset shining on a green velvet lawn, the sense of expectancy. It hadn't changed at all, I thought, as I sat there watching people assemble at Baltimore Memorial Stadium.

My mind ran back. Fifteen years ago to the month I stopped in London and heard Billy Graham in person for the first time at Wembley Stadium. It came at a crossroads in my life when, at age 29, I wondered what was the next step. I felt like one of the wandering nomads I had often seen in the Middle East, where I had lived for the previous three years, without roots, with no place that was mine.

Yet sitting high in the stands that night, I was one of the little candles Mr. Graham talked about, going out later into the darkness of the night.

My candle was aflame and it could never be blown out, not when God himself had lit it.

I wrote about that evening and timidly sent the story to *Decision*. Sherwood Wirt (discerning man!) saw some merit in it and published it several months later. Little did I know that my life was to be forever changed by that article. Ed Read read it and wrote to me. Our courtship by mail went from there.

And now, fifteen years later, as Ed's wife and the mother

of his children, I again went on Monday to another crusade in Baltimore, this time with the children along.

In a rather hard-boiled city it is astonishing and wonderful to see so many thousands going to hear the simple gospel. For simple it is. The music, the testimony of Joni Eareckson, Bev Shea's song, the choir, the message of Billy Graham, all is simplicity itself, not contrived, not phony, *the power of God unto salvation to every one who believes.*

It was youth night. Mr. Graham spoke on the prodigal son and had his own prodigal, Franklin, speak briefly before the message. It is helpful to know that even great men have wayward children, but God hears the prayers of parents.

At the invitation people began to move quietly forward. The children watched, wide-eyed. It is one thing to view the event on television. It is another to be there and see the vastness of the crowd and feel the holiness of that quiet moment.

I watched too through a blur of tears and thought how the scene has been repeated countless times. Candles were still burning in London after all these years and now thousands more were lit in Baltimore. No one can put out the light of the world burning in human hearts. It may tremble, flicker, falter, but it will not go out.

I know because mine is still burning.

July 27, 1981

The Lord *is* good. After writing a large check for our little Korean girl, I felt rather empty. There are doubts that arise at times and thoughts, unworthy ones, about all the things we could have done with that money. Another trip overseas, new furniture, carpet, even a gift to the church.

Then I sold two stories to magazines, which earn me scarcely more than minimum wage for the time invested, but are a nice lift nonetheless. And when I opened the June issue of *Guideposts*, I saw they were offering my book again, probably just to get rid of the last copies, but, being unexpected, that too cheered me.

July 29, 1981°

In my July bouquet, along with the roses, were two or three large blooms of Queen Anne's lace. Looking closely, I could see that every lace flower was made up of a multitude of separate blossoms, wee white petals and a tiny center. There were hundreds of miniscule flowers in each exquisite bloom.

"Why would God ever bother to create such detail in a flower-weed that might never be seen?" I asked Dad.

"So he can look at it and enjoy it," said he.

I could imagine God walking in the cool of the day through the fields and meadows and along roadsides looking at his garden. Seeing the lace, the little blue wild asters, the purple clover he had made, smelling wild roses and new-cut hay, hearing birds sing—how he must enjoy his creation!

I wonder, I wonder if I give him joy when he walks by me?

August 1, 1981

Ed took all three children to Friedens Chapel, (our first mission church) where the work seems at last to be winding

---

°This day's entry is adapted from my writing in *Daily Guideposts* (Guideposts: Carmel, N.Y., 1981), pp. 208-209.

down and the building ready for use in a few weeks. It was rather sweet to see them go. Susan was none too happy about it, but was persuaded to change to jeans and help. My quiet Ed works well with his hands and has helped there regularly these years. It is good for him to have an afternoon alone with the children, and it's good for me to be alone.

If only our little Anne were here. We've not heard a word more about when she might arrive.

We've picked blackberries lately, quarts and quarts of the biggest ones I've ever seen hanging in great clumps almost like grapes. I've cooked them and now have them dripping through a cheesecloth bag, the sweet essence of summer in rich, dark juice oozing through to be made into jelly. Some of the berries I put into pies which invariably boil over and set off the smoke alarm, but what yummy eating, especially with vanilla ice cream.

August 9, 1981

Otto Schumann, who read my *Guideposts* article about Jim Smith, was here for dinner and told us his story. Let me record it briefly. It is unique, but then so is everyone's. God never put anyone in a mold.

He was born into a cultured and wealthy family who came from Europe at the time of the Bolshevik Revolution. His great-grandfather, a brilliant musician, had played in the court of the last czar of Russia.

Otto's mother died when he was in sixth grade and his dad began drinking more heavily, leaving his two children to fend mostly for themselves.

Quite early Otto began to have an abiding interest in business, investing even his earnings from cutting grass in stock. His ambition was to become a millionaire.

After his marriage and the affluent lifestyle he and his wife adopted, his investments, and borrowings, became larger and larger. His head would fairly spin, manipulating the ups and downs of the market to make a profit both for himself and his clients.

It was too much. There were family tensions, then a divorce. To his amazement, Otto realized he had done what he vowed he'd never do: let an addiction—gambling—control him just as drinking had controlled his father.

Then, because of rising interest rates, a bearish market, and some misjudgments on his investments, his business world began to tumble around him. He had no place to turn, no wife, no parents, no friends, no God.

It was midwinter. The sidewalks of Reading were icy and the air frigid as he went home from his job for the last time. He flung himself into a chair and picked up the latest copy of *Guideposts* that his sister had subscribed for him. There he found the story of Jim Smith, maker of stoves, who lived in a suburb of Reading.

Jim had a deep faith, a peace that was lacking in Otto. It haunted him for weeks until he finally made an appointment to meet Jim.

As they visited, Otto told the whole sad tale of his failures, admitting he needed help desperately. He was at the end of himself.

Jim explained that only Christ could help him. He could call on Christ to wash away his sin, his failures, and make a new man of him.

And that's what Otto, weeping and sincere, did in Jim's office that day. The following Sunday he was in our church, where I met him.

The article I wrote had been such a struggle for me. But today, talking to Otto, I knew it was worthwhile.

August 22, 1981

I have forever left off being forty-three. From Mom and Dad came a gift along with a note, "It's not so nice to be reminded as to how old you are. Just remember you will never die."

Hope. What an inheritance to have.

Two weeks of vacation Bible school are now finished. Chris Dick was the director and, to my astonishment, she chose me to be her assistant. It was a new experience for me. Organization and administration are not my strongest points.

However, Chris has it in mind to make *me* director in a year or two. Utter panic seizes me at the thought. For one thing, I cannot cope with crafts: popsicle sticks, glue, bits of felt, and burlap all bore me. Providing refreshments, remembering first-aid kits, organizing schedules, classes, lessons, people—oh, the details make my head spin.

I must convince her it is not my calling. A writer-dreamer is not one to coordinate Bible school.

August 29, 1981

Early this summer Susan showed me a little Bible reading chart that she planned to follow, with her signature at the bottom verifying her decision. "God bugged me till I did it," she said, which is as apt a way as any to express godly conviction.

I was pleased. Yet I had no idea of the change it would make in her life. Having watched her go through a difficult year of moods, inexplicable surliness, uneven friendships, I assumed it was adolescent growing pains, something to be endured probably for two or three years at least.

Instead, this summer, the Word of God, living and powerful, changed her attitudes, her behavior, even her smile. *He sent his word, and healed them,* says the psalmist.

I told Susan I had seen a change in her since she began reading the Scripture each day.

"I know," she said. She had recognized it herself.

Mr. Taylor, our principal, was right. Two years ago he planned ten minutes into the school schedule each morning for a quiet time when the students read the Bible and pray. I told him then that you can't force spiritual growth, that lots of kids would waste the time. And many do. But there are also those who are forming the habit of seeking God every day, a habit, like brushing teeth, that can be learned only by daily practice until the day seems out of joint when one forgets. James, reading Isaiah each morning, is learning it. And now Susan.

Not always comprehending the meaning of the words, they still are submitting to God, recognizing his leadership first thing in the day. *Those that seek me early shall find me.*

September 5, 1981

It has become a Saturday morning ritual. On Friday evening I hear the three children discussing whose turn it is to go this week.

Early on Saturday, one of them stirs, has a quick wash, maybe, puts on old clothes, runs down the stairs, out the door, and across the road to Grampy's house for breakfast.

Now I have never been there, for I'm not invited. But

this is what I think happens. Gramp is always up early and sitting by the kitchen window praying, watching the birds in the maple, waiting. He welcomes the child, James, Susan, or Michael, warmly. Together they make breakfast: bacon, eggs, fresh orange juice, toast, tea, and once in a happy while, fried mushrooms.

At the table these two sit, savoring the food and talking lightly or seriously. They conclude with a reading from the Bible and a prayer. Maybe, if the day is good, they walk outside a little, under the trees, around the garden. Or they might ride bike. Then it's over.

Except for the memories.

September 14, 1981

She didn't get here in time for school, little Anne. I've been so hoping she would. Presumably six, she's never been to school at all. That means she will be an older child in her grade, and though at first it matters little, as children get older, it seems to worry them.

If she's coming, why can't it be now and not later? She is there in an orphanage, a child without a home who needs to be here, with us, as soon as possible. Does the agency bringing her try as hard as they might? They've had the check (which could have been earning high interest right now) all these months and we don't even hear from them. Or is it the government at either end? I wonder how long our application has lain in a heap on the desk of some bureaucrat who doesn't know that those papers represent a life, a child, hopeful and lonely, a child who was abandoned, without any known kin—except us.

She's ours and we've never even seen her.

Jesus is ours too, whom having not seen, we love.

September 23, 1981

Yesterday when I was all ready to call the agency about Anne and give them a piece of my mind, we received a phone call from our own local Tressler agency asking us to send a scrapbook of our family. For Anne. Surely it means she's coming *soon*, perhaps in weeks. Knowing a child's anticipation and elongated sense of time, no orphanage would show her a book of her new family unless she were soon to see us. It would simply be too much excitement and tension to bear for long.

So together, the kids and I (Ed at work), got pieces of construction paper and pasted photographs of our house, our church, ourselves, grandparents, Christmas trees, and such. There was a separate page for each family member, and opposite we wrote letters to her. Though she knows no English, someone can translate or at least tell her that we love her. We also stuck pieces of chewing gum, pencils, and barrettes on several pages.

What must go through the mind of a little girl as she thinks of a new home? Does she think often of the horror of being left in that inn a year ago, of never seeing again her parents or whoever it was she lived with? Does she wonder about us? Is she afraid? Will she like us?

We have a small photo of her. She looks like a small forlorn prisoner with her name pinned to her sweater. I long to put my arms around her.

October 20, 1981

The sun is touching the tips of the trees with gold as I look out the west window of the dining room. On the table a bouquet of zinnias are lit with color and roses the size of peonies. They belie the fact that it's mid-October.

I long to see Anne, yet in the middle of the night there comes an unwanted thought. The description of her translated into broken English, sounded as though she is slow, just able to count to ten but not, for instance, to distinguish colors. Even some of her personal habits sound more like a three-year-old than a six-going-on-seven child. Is the description accurate or is it even understated? Or has she simply regressed from all the trauma of the past year? What if she were retarded? Are we able at our age to commit ourselves to her for the rest of our lives? It is one thing to receive a handicapped child through birth, quite another to take one voluntarily. Would I be able to keep on working?

I'm not sure I could cope with this, complicated by the language and cultural differences. *What if I couldn't?*

I haven't mentioned it to Ed. It's just in the wee hours when I waken that it troubles me. But doubts are always dreadful then.

I can't and don't dwell on it. We have prayed too many years and have been led by God too clearly to go back. No man that puts his hand to the plow and looks back is worthy.

We must go forward in faith. If she is very slow, he will give us the grace to care for her. And if she isn't, how foolish my middle-of-the-night fretting will seem.

November 26, 1981

Our biggest event recently was a copy of a letter from the Justice Department saying, "Your cable was sent as requested." Whatever that means. A visa perhaps? There was no further explanation.

Then came a request for transportation money, which I

sent that same day. To think that the same book in which we began praying for another girl to come is the one whose profits are now providing the way for her to be here. How God works!

Susan has made a cuddly cat pillow to give her for Christmas and people at church are giving us used clothes. She simply *must* come before Christmas.

We'll be *parents* again. The agency must have winked at our ages. I gave Ed a Thanksgiving note today telling him I was especially thankful for him, my husband, for because of him, I have nearly everything else, the children, a warm, contented home, our old car kept in excellent repair by him, abundant meals, and love.

We had dinner at Russell's today, a most beautiful meal with all of Peg's lovely touches. Mom was seventy-eight on the tenth, a miracle lady indeed, as Marie McConaghay calls her, after all her illnesses.

December 16, 1981

Sitting here by our fragrant young spruce tree, I think of loved ones everywhere—in Missouri, Texas, Beirut, Ireland, London, Scotland, Washington, California, Cyprus, in all sorts of places, even Korea. For in Seoul lives our daughter, who has crept straight into our hearts though we've never seen her. This expectancy, this hope, makes that first Christmas seem so near, so real.

Apart from this prayer-about-to-come-true, we have had, in looking back, quite an ordinary year. Yet is it ever ordinary to have good health, to eat fresh-baked scone with marmalade and tea, to visit with dear friends, to go to church, to listen to a carol, to pick strawberries, to see the moon shining on snow? Is it ever ordinary to know him, our joy, our peace, our friend, our life?

These are extraordinary, priceless gifts from God, what gold cannot buy, and they are ours.

A lovely prayer I read recently fits my feeling tonight.

> Blessed Savior, Christ, most holy,
> > In a manger thou didst rest:
> Canst thou stoop again, yet lower,
> > And abide within my breast?

December 20, 1981

She's *coming*, Tuesday evening, to Philadelphia Airport directly from Korea, little Anne Marie, complete with jet lag, culture-shock, and homesickness. The phone call came this afternoon while I was visiting Aunt Ruth, and James called me there to let me know. What excitement and deep joy we've felt since.

This morning as the small ones in Sunday school gave their Christmas program and I saw Kim Taylor, I wept silently that Anne wasn't with them. I had nearly given up my prayer that she would be here in time for Christmas, nearly, but not quite.

Dear Hubby, he reminded me that maybe someone wiser than I timed her arrival, since Tuesday will be our last day of school before the holidays, giving us some time to get acquainted. While reading Luke 2 in preparation for the cantata in which he sings tonight, Ed said he saw a reminder of Anne. There was no room for Jesus except in hearts of folk who received him. What blessing he brought—and she must too! *Whosoever receiveth a little child in my name receiveth me.*

115

Love

---

*Behold, what manner of love the Father
hath bestowed upon us, that we should be
called the sons of God . . . .*

We loved Anne before she came. We loved her even
more after she came. What joy it was to hold her tight and
look at her vibrant smiling face.

Life without love would be bleak, utterly pointless,
without worth. I treasure the love of my husband, my
parents, my children, friends, students, neighbors, dear
ones everywhere who love me and whom I love.

But they pale beside the love of God who gave me his
dear Son, who though he was rich, yet for my sake became
poor, that I through his poverty might be *rich*.

Chapter

3

December 23, 1981

It was an evening to remember. At Philadelphia Airport we awaited the plane, Northwest Orient Flight 50, delayed for almost an hour. To fill the time, we walked around, fussed over our bag of clothes, watched planes, and tried to still the butterflies. James said it well, "It will never be the same again."

There was no turning back. We were bound to a child, a future—forever. We felt great joy and expectancy, but there was a certain fear too, a doubt that whispered, maybe you shouldn't have. What if you can't afford another? What if she can't learn well? How then will she even get English? Don't you have your hands full with these three?

And Faith answered, "Yes, all that may be true, but *God* is bringing her here."

As the plane taxied in, we were told that the children, two babies and our Anne, would come off last. The crowd milled around and suddenly in front of me, she stood shyly, taller than I thought, with the sweetest smile and two front teeth missing.

I reached for her and she flung her arms around me. It was all right. She was here, our *daughter*. I cried and laughed and handed her to Ed who simply beamed.

Anne walked out of the airport with us and never looked back. What tough resilience a child has to come through abandonment, orphanage life, a flight around half the world, then to step into a new family with perfect faith that all is well.

She sang and played and laughed all the way home. Ed's flashlight entranced her.

After a midnight supper of scrambled eggs and applesauce, her face sagged in weariness. *When* had this child begun her journey? Probably thirty hours earlier at least, maybe forty. I helped her take a bath and noticed her thin shoulders.

She was alseep in seconds in a temporary bed for her and Susan on the floor by the twinkling Christmas tree.

And there she lies this morning, still sleeping while Michael leans over her, thrilled to have a "little" sister. All three have been poking at her by spells, wanting her to waken. But, like a kitten, she rolls over and curls up again.

December 25, 1981

Christmas with a new daughter, herself our own gift, reminded us of that greater arrival so many years ago. We accepted her in faith, unconditionally, just as once we accepted Jesus. *As many as received him, to them gave he power to become the sons of God.* What a simple act it is to receive Jesus as Savior, yet how profoundly he changes us to be his child.

Several weeks ago I bought a doll, believing that she'd be here to receive it. And last night she did, with dear ones here to watch and laugh with her. She is such a busy child, perpetual motion, and has already thinned the doll's hair considerably with numerous shampoos.

Bedtimes are tricky. Anne cries then, a desolate, heartbroken cry which eases gradually when I lie down with her. I think then of all the horror of her abandonment and her cry when she discovered she was left behind.

January 2, 1982

Everyone has been in a balmy mood all week, beguiled as we are with Anne. James calls her his favorite little alien. She has the pinkest, hardest cheeks, like a plump pincushion. Time will bring its disillusionment, short tempers, quarrels when the real grain of the wood is bared without any shiny veneer. But until then, the mood here is delightful.

It required great thought to fit us all in. The tree came down a few days earlier than usual, and I set to with gusto, Ed wishing wistfully I would just put the girls in the living room in the bunk beds. But no, I had bigger plans than that. The children must have the bedrooms, and he and I would make do downstairs.

Forthwith we hauled down our double bed and promptly had an argument. In which corner of the living room shall we set it? I wanted it behind the door where it would show the least. Who wants to see a bed first thing in the living room? However, Ed wanted to move the least amount of furniture.

Hubby won, and it is now prominently placed just inside the door, destroying my pleasure in that room. Never mind. There are things that matter so much more, like not having a bed at all.

Russ and Peg, always generous, *gave* us their bunk beds for the boys, thus making more space in that tiny bedroom. The girls have the white twin beds in the big room along with all the other things that get thrown in, a sewing table, chest, filing cabinet, boxes, dressers, and such. And so, once again we fit snugly, six of us in a two-bedroom house. I do confess that I long for that "bigger house" that was part of my prayer along with Anne.

She is sleeping better now, the jet lag done, not up and down all night with great banging of doors, locking the bathroom, running back again to bed. The house vibrates when someone runs and I waken with a start.

I am tired and tense. How I look forward to some uninterrupted sleep.

January 13, 1982

A quiet, steady snow fell all day, cancelling school, an extra bonus since Anne was sick yesterday with high fever, and we all needed a day just to *be*.

There is a moment of truth on snow days, when listening to the dozens of cancellations on the radio of civic, religious, and social events. I realize there must be a lot of unnecessary activity in our lives, things we schedule but could very well do without. Some are canceled altogether and others postponed a month or two. In the meantime there is a wonderful, exhilarating freedom in this day with no slots of responsibility. One can slip into it all sorts of unexpected happiness—baking cookies, taking a walk in the snow, talking to neighbors (all of whom are out shoveling), reading stories to the children, listening to the *Messiah*.

Anne has had some hard, confusing, tearful days at

school, but with Mr. Taylor's kind help and her teacher, Miss Gossert, she is being fitted in nicely.

Nighttimes are hard and I must lie with her until she sleeps, sometimes quite a while. The bedroom is frigid and I lie there shivering though both girls are toasty warm. One of our economies is not to heat the bedrooms.

As I lie beside her, I often think of the months before she came, the anticipation, but also the foolish fears about her. Would she be difficult, hard to love, slow to learn? Would I regret all the money we had spent? Strange, un-trusting thoughts for one who believes God's will is in force. Now she is here, sweeter and more lovable than we dreamed, a priceless little girl, and all my fears have blown away like murky fog in a brisk north wind.

But then it's usually that way. Fears are phantoms. That's why God says over and over, "Fear not."

February 8, 1982

Sitting here, I am listening to a tape of a message from my past, Dr. Torrey of Calvary Church days, from Deuteronomy. He reminded me of the Israelites' shoes and clothes that lasted forty years in the wilderness, rather like our green carpet in the dining room. Or our old stove that just keeps on cooking and baking. And the house itself, how we keep fitting in one more. The walls must stretch.

Yet I hope, inside, that one day we'll have more space, room to make things pretty, less cluttered, a place to keep folks overnight, missionaries, friends, relatives.

Anne cried forty-five minutes this morning, Monday blues, I suppose. It turns out to be a pretty hectic scramble getting the lunches packed and all five of us out the door on time for school each day.

February 13, 1982

Blessed be Saturdays when there is no place to go. It has been a happy, contented day. I baked pies and Anne was pleased to make her own little one. Her English is incomparable, the first word being "i-da ca-deem," a four-syllable version of ice cream. Different from Susan, who has no sweet tooth at all, Anne loves the stuff.

She speaks less Korean now. Being a talker, she must have felt great loneliness at times, knowing we couldn't understand her, yet longing to express herself. At the dinner table she would tell long stories with gales of laughter and graphic sign language. The other three have picked up words, and together they speak a hilarious mixture of Korean and broken English. James especially talks just like her. What a racket they all make sometimes. Can one ever resign from motherhood?

March 7, 1982

It has rained, snowed, and iced all night and all day, a thoroughly messy, miserable weekend. I can tolerate it nicely in January when such things are ordained to be. But in March I feel it's, well, just out of season and not quite fair. Rain and wind and trickling waterways through the woods are more apt now. If only the kids could get outside.

There seem to be a thousand details to remember each week. Aunt Ruth's hip is healing well. Until she comes home, the kids and I visit her weekly at the Moravian Home and take care of her laundry, banking, and mail. Soon I must clean her house for her to return.

I've been asked to meet with someone once a week and counsel. People have heart-rending problems and need help. Yet, in this case, as in many others, it seems as though the need might be to *act* on counsel already given. It is easy to judge, not always wisely and kindly.

The tutoring I do on Mondays ran into a glitch, an unpleasantness with the child.

Ed's back has given him a fit, though it's improving now. I never saw him so immobilized before. He is always so active.

Speaking engagements are coming up. I must prepare, though I'm less than inspired.

Writing is largely neglected but on my mind all the time.

Ah, well, this month must pass. Spring is coming.

April 14, 1982

All month Anne has been saying, "Happy birthday, seben, tomorrow." She is thrilled to be having a birthday, the day before Michael's, in fact. It is the day given on her passport (April 22), an educated guess, for no one really knows. Mike and she are rather tickled to be back to back.

Her memory is quick. Often she tells me things I thought would have blurred in all the excitement, about the Christmas tree, her new pajamas which she wore that first night, even her first midnight meal.

In stark contrast to the joy and excitement over our children, the sheer satisfaction they give us now, there is heartache, confusion, a groping for stability in the family of some I love dearly. For them, it is uncertainty. (*How* does one act with a child who is done with home?) And also a sense of failure and guilt. (Where did we go wrong?)

There is more than one way to lose a child. Elizabeth is gone, but she is safe. Death is terrible, but a clean and somehow honorable break. A rejection of parent by child or of wife by husband is messy, unnatural, devastating.

I am praying constantly for these who suffer such.

May 9, 1982—Mother's Day

This morning Anne, looking like a peach blossom, was dedicated in church along with us, her parents, in a lovely and moving ceremony. Usually babies are given by their parents to God. Today we acknowledged that this beautiful little girl is first his, then ours.

She wore the pink dress which I had once *planned* for Elizabeth, then got instead a year later for Susan. In a sense it symbolizes all three daughters, one of them already with God, the others loaned to us for a while.

May 12, 1982

The hill is bereft. This morning Ed left for his annual pilgrimage to Missouri, and tonight Mom and Dad are boarding the plane in New York for Ireland. After three years of planning and being deterred by Mom's illnesses, they are going as happily as once they went on their honeymoon.

Yesterday Ed and the three eldest got 350 pounds of horseradish root stock in Baltimore for him to plant on the farm, an acre or so. It is an experiment of his to see if he can get something profitable going there.

Tonight with folk scattered abroad, I sit here and look at the bouquet of roses Russ gave Mom for Mother's Day. She left them here with us this morning. I pray especially for him and for all my dear ones who need God's special touch tonight, for comfort, for gladness, for safety.

May 20, 1982

Anne's face lit up last evening and she exclaimed,

"Anne-little-boy-play-airport." Over and over it she went, concluding happily, "Daddy, Mommy, Susan, Michael, James, Anne-airport-little boy."

It didn't take any effort to figure out what she wanted. Obviously she is happy here and now would like a playmate her size. All we need is to go to the airport and pick one up. Would that it were so simple (and so inexpensive)!

Another child. Wait till Ed hears that!

As for me, I've about concluded that I'm getting too old for any more. Anne, bouncing ceaselessly, laughing, chattering, is part of us, an answer to prayer. But I have been worn to a frazzle at times with all four of them.

How wonderful spring is!

June 15, 1982

It is good for a child to be deprived often of television, of soda pop and candy, of foolish, vain literature.

It is not good to be deprived of loving, respectful attention, family laughter, homemade meals, mom in the kitchen, dad puttering around his car.

Housecleaning officially began today, a job which always takes longer than I wish. I'm wild to do some writing, but cannot settle to that till I get my house in order. Susan is a real help.

Ed is putting in a new plumbing system of plastic pipe, one of the thorough jobs he does when he sets his mind. He and the kids have been digging a trench across the yard for the pipe. I'm glad he is teaching the boys how to work with their hands, to plumb, to dig, to change the oil in the car.

He's a good and dear father. We are safe with him.

June 30, 1982

Is there anything quite so marvelous, so utterly delightful, as a lightning bug? Tonight on the way home from church, Anne and I watched them in the meadows along the Pool Forge Road. When she got home, she and Ed caught one and put it in a jar. I remember doing that as a child, running around our yard on a memorable summer evening with Russell.

I wonder why God made lightning bugs. Harmless, peace-loving little things, they seem to spread only happiness and goodwill. Was it for his own good pleasure? To make children laugh and run?

July 3, 1982

Recently in my great burden for special loved ones, it came to me that I should pray and fast one day a week. Could I do it? I wondered. Food is one of my chief delights.

The thought would not leave, however, and so I've been fasting once each week, not eating after supper on Friday until twenty-four hours later on Saturday evening.

I've found that though there is a heaviness, there is also a wonderful intimacy with God and a clarity and perspective on matters of the Spirit.

Today was such a day.

August 10, 1982

We are nestled back home, finally coming out of the chaos that seems to accompany a trip. One wonders about vacations—two weeks to plan and prepare, two weeks traveling, two weeks more to recover, do laundry, catch up on the garden—and that's the summer mostly gone.

We drove to Missouri on what seemed to me to be the two hottest days of summer. I felt positively *cooked* in the middle of the front seat with no air-conditioning.

Along the way I wondered, has anyone got a fifteen-year-old, 240,000-mile car going on a trip across the country with four kids? Not many, for sure. Yet we sailed along quite happily, the motor quieter than many newer cars, thanks to Ed's excellent care.

Good friend Wynona Probert took all of us in, and she and Don made us feel completely at home. Ed worked long hours with his horseradish while I mostly did what I do at home, took care of the family.

The second week we stayed with the Estes and Harrington families, Ed's cousins in Carthage. There was a brief visit with Evelyn and George, who recently had a heart attack, but is joyful and loving as always. How the children enjoyed Uncle George's pool.

The trip home was pleasant and, thankfully, cooler.

September 28, 1982

Tonight at the table Anne said, "Jesus in my heart, heben."

"Oh," I said, "Jesus is in your heart?"

She nodded.

"And now you're going to heaven?"

She paused thoughtfully. "Not today," she said.

She had breakfast with Mom on Saturday when Dad was away. Mom was talking to her about how God made trees, grass, flowers, clouds, and, well, just everything in the world. Anne chimed in reciting, "God so lubbed da world . . ." which touched Mother—that this small alien already knows the greatest fact in the world.

How she memorizes Bible verses, great long ones at school. And she can say the books of the Old Testament.

To think that I once feared she couldn't learn!

October 7, 1982

A sweet young thing at Yoder's market wondered today, while we stood at the checkout, if I was doing another book. I've had many thoughts about it though my creative urge seems to have been drained lately with my Saturday prayer burden.

A sequel, perhaps. Yet there is always the soul-searching. How much do I expose my children, for instance, or Ed? How much must I reveal for it to be honest? Do I obscure and disguise things that are heartbreaking, that hurt deeply, but that might be helpful to another?

There are many things to consider. I cannot jeopardize family relationships, nor can I pretend that we are what we are not. That is the dilemma in writing about one's family and self.

I must pray. Meanwhile I'll go on trying to sort and polish my other manuscripts which heretofore have not captured an editor's fancy.

October 8, 1982

While I played the new organ at Mom's, the children gathered around, pushing the buttons, listening, singing. How *beautiful* is the hymn "Jesus, Lover of My Soul" and that forgotten one, "Where Jesus Is, 'Tis Heaven There." How is it that we hear these so seldom? Are our tastes warped from all the current, repetitious whining we hear today?

As I played, it came to me that memories may be what

hold a child steady while growing older. When one wanders, as may happen, even for a *short* time (I pray), there must be something for that person to *miss*, to remember with longing in the low places of life. That's what the prodigal son did. He came to himself and remembered his father's house and all that was there.

Probably our chief task as parents, Ed and I, is to fill our children's lives with such love and laughter, gracious hymns, Bible verses, meals eaten in harmony, a sense of safety, that if they go to that far country and waste their living, they will have something to remember and, God willing, to come back to.

October 14, 1982

On Tuesday I came home from school to find my story of Otto was returned, a flat rejection. The reasons seemed flimsy in the letter. Even Ed had thought it a good story, and I was really hurt.

Then in my misery, I suddenly remembered a prayer I had made some weeks ago while fasting one Saturday, that I was willing even to sacrifice my writing for as long as God saw fit if it would help the one for whom I prayed. It was a hard prayer. Writing is such a part of me, and harder yet to experience when my story was rejected Tuesday.

Yesterday, asking that God remove any presumption from me, I did offer all my rejections past and future to him who chooses foolish and weak things, even things which are *not*, that he might have the glory. I pray that they will be a sweet savor to him and a rebuke to that evil one.

October 21, 1982

We have had a new experience at our house recently.

For the first time in years, Ed is on day work regularly. That means he is home every evening, a wonderful thing for our children as they grow older, not to mention the advantages for Ed himself. I often wished when they were small and so *busy*, that he could be here to help read to them, bathe them, play games, wipe up spilled milk, and such.

Now that he is here, I've had to get used to it and remember not to make plans that exclude him, such as having Betty Ann here (not that he minds; she does) or running over to Russ and Peg's for an evening.

Today the neighbor children were here again after school for Good News Club. Ed good-naturedly endures the noisy arrival, snacks for all, then enforced quiet for the family as I tell stories and teach a Bible verse. We finally have a belated supper of hamburgers.

My day seems much easier now that supper is not at a rigid time. And Hubby must enjoy having his evenings with us.

December 29, 1982

All six of us went to Lancaster County Courthouse this afternoon and waited nervously for the court to convene. At the appointed time we went into the courtroom, rising as Judge Appel appeared and called into session Orphan's Court. It was easier this time and questions seemed fewer.

I thought of the prayers, in faith, that began years ago, just after Anne was born, though we didn't know it then. We asked for a little girl we had never seen and often wondered if we ever would find her. I thought too of the months of uncertainty as we waited, in hope, for her arrival, and that expectant, joyful day just a year ago when she stood before me at the airport. And today, I reached my arm around her in love as she sat, remarkably still, beside me in the courtroom.

It was over. The judge smiled benignly and congratulated us. Lee Kyung Sun is now Anne Marie Kyung Read.

Faith, hope, and love are full circle now.

January 10, 1983

An annual highlight of Ed's year is the Harrisburg Farm Show. He has taken the children every year even when they had to be carried. Today Susan chose not to go, Mike was sick, but James and Anne went with him. She loved it.

It would seem, reflected Ed, that her parents, whoever they were, must have had intelligence, beauty, and a sense of pride and culture. How else could they have produced this eager, beautiful child? And if that is so, then why did they give her up? Were they ill? Were they dead and her relatives couldn't care for her? Did they fall into hard times and think that by giving her up, she would be better off?

We'll probably never know. Occasionally she talks about her "mother," though it seems to be anyone who cared for her along the way. But sometimes the stories, broken and mixed up and confused with bad dreams, sound tragic. And when she cries, I still hear the heartbreak that must have overwhelmed her when she found herself abandoned, utterly alone.

February 10, 1983

Jack, one of the most charming rascals I've had in school recently, sat at his desk, head forward, concentrating, a rare occupation for him. I paused and looked over his shoulder. He grinned sheepishly.

"What's that, Jack, a poem?"

He nodded.

"Did you write it?"

"Yes, ma'am."

I couldn't believe it. Jack, writing a poem, of all things.

"Would you let me read it?" He was obviously embarrassed, yet I sensed he wanted me to see it. Reading it, I nearly cried.

> I'm all alone
> I have no playmates
> no brothers nore sisters my age.
> My Dad's to bigg for me
> hes got lots of work to do
> We hardly never play games at all.
> So I'm so upset inside
> but I'll never show it at all
> I'm so alone I need
> someone to hold me
> tite and to love me hard.
> Will you be my friend.

I wonder what his busy, prosperous father would say if he read it, misspelling and all. How poor in spirit is a child whose parents overlook him.

February 19, 1983

I have been rereading S. D. Gordon's *Quiet Talks on Prayer*, a classic that I profit from over and over. These past months of concentrated prayer and weekly fasting have made me keenly aware of the principalities and powers, the spiritual wickedness in high places. Prayer is a battle, often protracted, against that evil one. For the first time in my life, I have sensed strongly the power of Satan and his hosts. Yet *greater is he that is in me than he that is in the world.* All the forces of evil cringe before the name of Jesus, that is above all names.

The moral power of prayer is beyond measure, far greater than the physical or military strength of even the strongest army.

Daniel prayed three weeks, discovering that the one who brought the answer had been delayed by demonic forces. I think of that often as I pray. It is a battle, intense and wearisome, but it is the *only* way to do anything that matters, anything that will last.

As the hart panteth after the waterbrook, so panteth my soul after thee, O God. There is an insatiable longing to know God, and in the very longing complete satisfaction. Is this what heaven is? To be forever thirsty and to have that thirst forever slaked?

April 27, 1983

Last week in a three-day spring vacation, we drove southward to Williamsburg, Virginia, leaving a fresh snowstorm here. Arriving that evening, we found a motel, then drove past the lovely campus of William and Mary to the old town. There we walked up and down the beautiful colonial street with the lamps aglow, the windows warm and inviting as we looked in, the taverns busily serving dinner. It was an enchanting moment, with all the beauty of history and none of its squalor and sorrow.

The next morning we visited Carter's Grove, a vast, elegant estate nearby, to be used a month hence as a meeting place for President Reagan and other world leaders in an economic conference. The rest of the day we toured the town, the mansions, craft shops, the Capitol. Early spring in Virginia is exquisite.

The following morning we began our trip home along the James River, stopping at several plantations. My favorite was Westover, a handsome house of casual elegance with several dogs and kids' toys lying about.

James especially is enamored of these large houses and wants to live on the James River someday. He has for years been designing his big house, a Georgian one. It is fun to have dreams, preposterous ones, which inevitably get modified over the years, yet they are often fulfilled in strange ways by God.

May 7, 1983

Recently I've come to see again that privacy is not all it appears to be. For years now, current thinking has promoted the notion that children, that all of us, in fact, need great privacy, private bedrooms, private baths, basement playrooms cut off from the rest of the house, personal televisions, telephones, stereos with headsets. Might it not be considered that all sorts of mischief could be prevented were people to share their quarters a bit more?

How, for example, can a child hide drugs, cigarettes, pornography, and such if there are one or two younger siblings in the same room? It is not impossible, but surely would be much harder to manage. How can a teenager listen to frenzied music late at night if another is there wanting to sleep? Why do we think a child alone should bear the responsibility of choosing his or her own entertainment? What are parents for if not to guide? Further, how are children to learn to share if they have their own of everything? No wonder so many are demanding their rights. Is *anyone* learning about sacrifice?

I must admit I am often tired of our crowded, untidy house. On the other hand, I can now appreciate the warmth, the loving camaraderie, the sheer fun and safety of being so close.

June 17, 1983

These mornings the birds begin shortly after 4:30 with a triumphant opening chorus as though the great conductor raised a baton and gave the downbeat to begin. Otherwise, how would they all know to begin at once? Who, but God, could synchronize such a multitude of music?

I listen in bed, marveling, then drift off as it softens and the birds look for their breakfast.

Today I began work at Shady Maple Farm Market from noon till nine tonight, tomorrow for five hours. I feel a little apprehension and, I must admit, a shade of humiliation. After all, several of my students work there. What if they perform better than I do? It's such a busy place. Suppose I can't keep up? Why should I weigh apples and artichokes when I'd rather write?

The children aren't quite sure about it. Not since they were small and I did substitute teaching have I left them behind. James is worrying for me. I told him you don't get paid for worry.

The housecleaning is nearly finished. The kids helped me paper the girls' bedroom and it is fresh and bright and feminine. I remember papering it eleven years ago with three little busybodies underfoot, snipping, tasting the paste, walking off with my tools. Elizabeth trimmed half her hair at that time, looking adorably lopsided.

This time I leaned hard on them for help.

June 20, 1983

A wet morning, the second one, but I've sat here (early) and thought of the glory of God. At times there comes an overwhelming desire to see and know him face-to-face.

I read again this poem by Amy Carmichael of wonderful expectancy.

> Do we not hear Thy footfall, O Beloved,
> > Among the stars on many a moonless night?
> Do we not catch the whisper of Thy coming
> > On winds of dawn, and often in the light
> Of noontide and of sunset almost see Thee?
> > Look up through shining air
> And long to see Thee, O Beloved, long to see Thee,
> > And wonder that Thou art not standing there?
>
> And we shall hear Thy footfall, O Beloved,
> > And starry ways will open, and the night
> Will call her candles from their distant stations,
> > And winds shall sing Thee, noon, and mingled
> > light
> Of rose-red evening, thrill with lovely welcome;
> > And we, caught up in air,
> Shall see Thee, O Beloved, we shall see Thee,
> > In hush of adoration see Thee there. °

And yet, there was a sense too of sin this morning, of thoughtless words to Mom, to Russell, to Ed, to Grandma Read, to others over the years. What can wash away my sins? Nothing but the blood of Jesus. To be forgiven—is there a word so beautiful?—of all my sin. That's why I *can* see him one day so joyfully.

° *Gold Cord* (S.P.C.K., 1952), p. 274.

June 28, 1983

Is there anything so sensuous as a summer evening? I sit in the backyard and watch the sun loll behind the tree line while the moving branches brush the clouds, pink and gold, across the west.

There is the scent of new-mown grass, and roses, a hint of onions in the garden, the horsey odor from the neighbor's meadow. The dusk falls as lightly as dew, the birds sing lullabies, and the evening star, a greater light, appears, while around me a host of lesser lights flicker. Who, but God, would ever have thought of a lightning bug?

The children roll and romp in the grass, then come and sit by me, feeling the hush and perhaps a bit of awe. White petunias glow like galaxies of stars in the flower beds. At last it is dark.

July 7, 1983

Three years ago today we flew to London. And right now, I am using that diary in some writing, making me very nostalgic. This season is for dreaming anyway on warm sleepy afternoons or long twilights, of trips, of bigger houses, even of a different car. I get caught up in wishing, then have to turn it into a prayer.

One of my strongest yearnings is again my writing. After the strange Lent I observed from any sustained writing over this past year, I have apparently regained my creative urge. The consuming, constant prayer burden is less oppressive now. I do not weep so easily, and perhaps this has made room for the other. Fasting has been interrupted by my weekend work at Shady Maple, but I have in no way ceased from praying. There is still a vast unhappiness, a hollowness in the one for whom I pray, that only Christ can fill, that God-shaped vacuum which is in everyone's soul.

July 11, 1983

Anne's prayer tonight: "Thank you for lunch and nice pie Mom make. Thank you for President Reagan; he getting old. Thank you for Pastor Dick; he teach good. Thank you for bishionaries Mike and Elsie Lyth and Jonas and Sadie Stoltzfus, going back."

Sometimes she says she will go to Korea and be a missionary. Her perceptions are very sweet.

July 15, 1983

Ed, usually an abstainer, is experimenting with coffee these days. Today, earlier than I care to think about, he crashed through the door, which tends to stick. I was happily catching a few extra winks. He asked where the "little coffee maker" was.

I told him, then listened to great rumblings in the kitchen, musing, as I drifted off to sleep, how men can make such a racket.

Crash. I jumped as he came through the door again. This time he wanted the "little coffeepot," a different utensil altogether. The first request had been a mistake, he said sheepishly.

"You used it just a couple days ago," I grumped. "It's wherever you left it." Which is the classic wifely response.

Knowing full well he'd not find it himself, I staggered out to the kitchen, found it immediately, and flounced back to bed. In moments I smelled the coffee.

What was the use? I got up.

July 27, 1983

After days of hearing odd sounds, in the toaster it seemed, behind my head, I changed my reading position at the table early in the morning to see if there were leprechauns moving in with us. Soon the most cunning little mouse scurried along the shelf and looked at me with his shiny black eyes. Then with a flick of his tail, he was down inside the toaster eating the crumbs. When I got up to watch, he leaped out and rushed back to his hole behind the stove somewhere.

Such a friendly little fellow, it seemed a shame to set a trap. But when the bag of rice leaked all over the floor, I knew the mouse had to go.

July 29, 1983

Some weeks ago Hubby began to work on our north basement room, just a dreadful black hole with old insulation, like Spanish moss, hanging down in humid strips from the ceiling. What began as a simple repair has turned into a major job. He replastered the walls, put in new insulation, and built a wooden ceiling. His plans are to build shelves and install a sump pump to drain out water. One thing seems to lead to another. With whitewash and paint, it is not recognizable as the same place.

Mom heard about a used freezer that we bought for fifty dollars. It works perfectly. I am happily occupied in filling it with berries, beans, and corn.

My prayer for a bigger house—could this be it? Not at all what I thought of or hoped for, but then, sometimes prayers are answered that way. We'll be able to store many things there, relieving some of the congestion upstairs. We *could* put our bed there and restore our living room to what it once was, but I don't relish using the outside entrance in the winter!

August 9, 1983

It has been a new experience to have Ed in the hospital. He felt chest pains, quite severe ones, in church on Sunday, then they subsided. Loretta Eberly was here for dinner, but I noticed Ed lay down after eating lightly.

Later he drove himself to the hospital emergency room just to be checked. An hour later the doctor phoned me and calmly said he was in the Intensive Care Unit. I felt shock: what had they *done* to him? He left here driving.

Since then, he has left the ICU and is taking medicine for an ulcer. Too much horseradish, maybe! It is a great relief to have something so manageable as that.

In heartbreaking contrast, a young man at church, Curtis Hoke, who was to be married in three weeks to one of our teachers, Carol Stoltzfus, broke his neck diving and is now a quadriplegic. In one split second everything changed. *Who hath known the mind of the Lord? or who hath been his counsellor?*

And I think again of Marie's continuing grief over Dennis, who was recently moved to a place that would break any mother's heart. I remember when he was as fine and dear as James or Michael.

Marie told me once that God had given her a clear sense of Dennis well and whole one day in heaven. Hope. It is that that keeps her steady and sweet. I look at her and see the gold shining through the cauldron of constant grief. As Amy Carmichael says, that gold is Christ.

Ed is coming home tomorrow. How rich we are.

142

September 12, 1983

It is still hot, today the forty-sixth day with temperatures soaring over ninety. And not only hot but exceedingly dry, the famous Lancaster County corn is parched and rattling in the wind.

The summer ended in a whirl of canning—tomatoes, dill pickles, relish—and arranging the new basement room. How wonderful to have a junk room besides the girls' bedroom.

I'm enjoying school again with my thirty-four senior high students. Susan is deep into volleyball, ecstatic to be named one of two outstanding players in a tournament on Saturday. She is agile, quick, never awkward.

Michael, who grew up without making much noise, entered *seventh* grade. I rely on him more and more for help, which he gives willingly. He's a quiet boy with a fine touch on the piano. At school he and Peter Steiner are buddies, both peacemakers in the rather tempestuous football games the boys play.

James, who obviously has my dim outlook on sports, has decided he really ought to join the soccer team again. He cares so little about practices, games, or results, yet feels he has let himself and others down when he doesn't take part. So he sturdily went to practice after we managed to get a pair of soccer shoes at this late date.

All the money and energy spent on games, on uniforms, officials, equipment, gyms, awards! One wonders: is it for what is *best*, or only good? The kids practice and travel long hours, and sometimes it seems to be part of the family breakup that everyone bemoans. Are we caught into something bigger than we thought?

October 10, 1983

Susan came in with an exquisite, tiny bird that she found in the woods. Terrified, unable to fly, it nestled in my hand, a warm place, and shut its eyes in contentment. I could nearly hear it purr.

We gave it water and tried to feed it, not too successfully, keeping it overnight in a shoebox. Such a fetching little scrap it was that during my quiet time this morning, I set it on the table and watched it hop about, certainly not concentrating very well on my devotions.

Still, I remembered that not a sparrow falls but God sees. As Ed left for work, he said, "You can't get much leaster than that."

October 26, 1983

During our special meetings at church, I invited everyone to go that I could think of in our neighborhood. They all with one accord made excuses, most of them good ones. I understand. People are busy today. Yet I was disappointed. I've prayed years for my neighbors, some of them.

Then on Sunday morning in pouring rain, Peg Elmer phoned and wondered if I'd take five (five?) children, assorted ones, her own and others, along to church.

I sent the menfolk on in the pickup, while Susan and I stuffed everyone else in the car, eight of us.

They all seemed to like Sunday school. I noticed again that Danielle listened attentively to the evangelist. This special friend of Anne's has always been a responsive child in my Good News Club.

Then tonight she returned the jars in which I had given them soup during their mother's recent illness. Would she go along to church to the special youth groups? She would.

144

On the way home she told me she had asked Jesus to be her Savior tonight.

Another least one. I must admit I felt a moment of disappointment last Sunday when no one went with us but some *children. Take heed, that ye despise not one of these little ones,* said Jesus.

November 6, 1983

Churchtown is beautiful all the time, but surely the autumn is the most charming season of all. Every day the children and I admire the homes, the brown stone church in the center of town, the lovely views over the valley on either side. The houses are old, large, mellow, and with the golden leaves and blue sky of fall, as beautiful as Williamsburg.

For the past year one of the houses has been for sale, a gray stone one with red shutters, a handsome front door, and a sun porch facing west. I must have dreamed of that house every day this past year. Ed harrumphed when I mentioned it, but the children and I pretend it is ours as we go by.

Today James wanted to take photographs of local scenes, and I suggested we stop and look at "our house," since it is empty. We did, peering in the windows. There is an elegant living room with a marble fireplace, large windows, and a wide staircase. How lovely it would look at Christmas.

There are things that matter so much more, and so I try not to think about it too much.

But how I enjoy dreaming as I drive by each day.

November 13, 1983

Hubby's birthday and a happy one it was with Dave and

Charlotte Saint and part of their family here. I had roast chicken and all the fixin's along with pie, Ed's favorite, instead of cake for dessert.

His ulcer, more a nuisance than a great problem, is slowly mending. Actually the physical, for which we expend great thought and effort, is less important than mental-emotional health and certainly less than our spiritual well-being. And if we only knew it, caring for the spiritual and mental guarantees better physical health. *Seek ye* first *the kingdom of God, and his righteousness; and all these things shall be added unto you.*

Since summer, Ed and I have been reading the Bible and praying together each morning at 6:15 before he goes to work. It is brief, often sleepy, but still a sweet time of bowing before God, the one who glues marriages and families together.

I thank God for Ed's integrity, his moral character, his loyalty, the fine example he is to our children. *The steps of a good man are ordered by the Lord.*

November 17, 1983

Sitting here in school as the day begins, I look around at my students. Each in his place during this brief devotional period, with head forward, and reasonably quiet. Some are praying, some are faking, a few sleeping.

While they are still, I pray also for them. They're a great bunch.

There is Dick with his deformities: cleft palate, deafness, halting speech. Help him, Lord, especially in his math today.

Beside him is William, the silent macho type who leads others. He's learning to make right choices and calls Jesus his best friend now. May that always be so.

Be with Melanie today, Lord, so fiercely independent and shy. She never asks for help, but I believe she longs for love, even mine, at times.

My explosive boy, Josh. He needs a balm for his disturbed, inner self. May he learn self-control, that gift of your Spirit. May his dad love him.

For our newest student, Janice, who loves you deeply and feels out of step with others who love you less. It's hard to be a misfit when you're sixteen.

Crystal, sweet, pretty, yet so limited. Today we'll work on those multiplication tables once more. Help her, Lord, to remember how to tell time.

The pastor's kid, always scrutinized, is such a likable, good-natured boy. He loves to help people. Help him not to overload his circuits.

And then, Father, there's Kelly Ann, who has no earthly father; does she know you? And Brad with CP. And Lewis, who has not met you yet; he sits reverently at least. Loris, friendly, open, and utterly pure in spirit. Ted, whose mom is so ill; he must ache often.

These and all the others, Lord. Time is gone, but I lift each one with their unspoken fears, disappointments, burdens to you to bless this day.

November 30, 1983

I have to admit defeat. As a mother of middle age, I am incapable, utterly unable to shop for teenagers. Gone forever are the days when I'd walk around town, pick up all sorts of bargains, bring them home, and they'd not only fit, but be greatly appreciated.

So—this year I let Susan and James shop with me and

choose their own Christmas gifts. This year Mr. Taylor lets me leave school at noon on Wednesdays, so today I took James with me. We went to Park City, had a leisurely snack, then browsed and bought. He has a good eye for clothes, expensive taste (though not always indulged), and a knowledge of fabrics and brands.

Last week Susan and I went. We dithered over leather boots. Realizing she'd have no money left for anything else, she chose instead a marvelous red dress, among other things. I've had to persuade her that red is one of her colors, not the quiet browns and blues she has thought suited her. When she tried on the dress, she knew it was beautiful.

Recently at school she gave up the touch football she has played for years with a gang of boys, suddenly grown big. Admitting that it probably wasn't appropriate to play any longer with them in such a game, she now watches and cheers. Actually, I think she feels a measure of relief that she can get on with being a girl.

May she always be as tender and discreet and lovely inside as she is now.

December 25, 1983, Christmas

The cold is bitter, the ground snow-covered, but our spirits are warm. Some dear ones were unable to come last evening, but Dad led Mom and all the aunts here one by one, no small task with the snow and icy wind. We had high tea—soup, fruitcake, cookies, breads, and then Anne, her face shining, said, "My heart so 'cited, my I open gifts?"

She might. The best ones were boxes—she adores them. One a little treasure box of chocolates, the other a lovely old one of bygone days from Aunt Ruth, the third a sewing box from Grammy, something Anne has longed for.

This morning with the bitter cold the car wouldn't start, so we couldn't go to church. I spent the time cooking, enjoying immensely the preparation of food for those I love best. Such wonderful scents, the ham sizzling in the oven and the yeasty odor of hot rolls rising, all mingled with our hemlock tree. And colors, golden sweet potatoes and green cole slaw, Aunt Dee's chow-chow, fruit salad brought by Aunt Ruth.

How dreadful if one had no food on such a day, or any day. I think of Sudan and Chad and other places where hunger has been so long.

Russell missed the dinner and we missed him. He had to answer a call to repair a heater in one of his rented houses. Later he came and all of us sat through the evening reminiscing. Dad read to us from John 1: *The Word was made flesh, and dwelt among us, (and we beheld his glory).*

What wonder this, that God became like us, so that we might be like him!

December 27, 1983

James says Anne measures 6.5 on the Richter scale, an apt description.

At the dinner table tonight, she said she had lived in four "countries," meaning four homes. Between bites of food, she told us more than she ever has about her past.

Her first mommy bled terribly, she said, and died. She has mentioned this before, what must be a horrifying memory. I would guess it was her real mother. Was it through childbirth, a hemorrhaging illness, an accident of violence? As she gets older, she may piece it together.

Her next mommy she *lost*, she said, and laughed apologetically as though it were her fault. That must have been when she was left at the inn and no one ever came back for her. Perhaps the one in whose custody she was—an aunt, cousin, neighbor—was simply unable to care for her and thought it better to leave her. What must a child feel when no one, *no one* is there?

At the third place, she told us, there were many children and a big house, obviously the orphanage. There she lived nearly a year before she came to us. The care was good, but being the youngest, she was often lonely, since she was the only one of them that did not go to school.

Now she is with us. One would think that with four upheavals in probably two years, a child would be timid, fearful, stunted emotionally. That Anne is whole and joyful, beautiful in face and spirit, is a tribute to God who kept her that way when we prayed—and when we didn't. Her name, Kyung, means "brightness."

I have learned, again, that I can depend on God to give us our dream-prayers in his own time and way. Anne came to us; that prayer was wonderfully answered. She is here, a live, bouncing, tangible proof of God's sovereign care. But there are other requests, other burdens, for which I still await an answer, some too personal even to record on these pages, but which I believe he will fulfill.

The Greatest of These Is Love

As the Father hath loved me, so have I
loved you; continue ye in my love.

The teen years rolled along, years that I heard would be exasperating, perplexing, fearful. Would our training and love be derailed?

So far it has not been that way, all thanks to God. There was occasional turbulence, but the overwhelming mood of these years was joy, laughter—and love. The children in their gradual maturing became friends and companions. We liked being together. Mealtimes when we were a whole family were a special pleasure.

How gracious God is to us, that he has given us this greatest of gifts. We thank him, knowing that each day of contentment and happiness is indeed a gift, a jewel to be treasured, knowing also that in this fallen world, we would still have heartache and bitter disappointments. Our faith is not in our children but in our God, to whom we have committed them.

Chapter

4

January 21, 1984

After a week of worthless mail, I threatened to get a new mailman as Ed came in from the post office. He handed me another pile of what looked like junk. Hidden in the middle, however, was a big envelope from Evelyn Bence at *Today's Christian Woman*. It contained some of my stories, which she was returning, but it also had a check for an article I wrote *years* ago and recently refurbished. It was based on a second- or third-grade essay by James called "The Most Wonderful Place on Earth." To him it was, and probably still is, *Home*.

It was a great lift to my spirits to have it accepted, this on one of the coldest mornings of the year, around zero, with an early morning moon shining on snow and a cold brittle day of sunshine.

My Saturday fasting seems to be often interrupted lately for one reason or another. But, oh, I do pray with all my heart, that the one for whom I've had this great burden, would know and love the Lord Jesus with all his heart. It would make such a difference.

January 28, 1984

Since last year, our church has been collecting money to build an addition, called a Family Center, to our present building. Among other things, it will include a gym. Susan is thrilled about that.

Pastor Dick, wise man that he is, has insisted we pay cash as we go, so a sizable sum must be there before we even start. It seemed a phenomenal amount to raise, and yet we will soon have two-thirds of it, cold cash in the bank drawing interest until we start. How much more sensible than borrowing money and then for years paying back both interest and principal, along with recriminations about the large debt, backbiting, maybe even a church split with a few left to carry the load. Waiting is an exercise in faith, waiting for God to supply in his time, not necessarily ours.

The Avian flu has decimated flock after flock of Lancaster County chickens lately, a real disaster for the area. Recently, good friends, Monroe and Mim Good, lost 60,000 birds. Their chicken house had to be cleaned, sterilized is closer to the truth, and much help was needed.

Ed, always conscious of farmers and the vagaries of their jobs, took the three older children over to help one long day. It was not a pleasant job. But then, he wanted them to learn to help someone even when it's not fun, without pay.

March 1, 1984

Last Saturday we all went to the basketball tournament at Lancaster where our school, along with four others, was playing. Our teams didn't win, not in the most points, but then that's not the only way to win.

As they began to hand out the sportsmanship awards, I

leaned over to Ed and whispered, "That's the best one to get." He nodded.

Just then Susan's name was called as the one girl to receive it. Being her mother, I thought she deserved it, but I was touched, nonetheless, and watched her receive it with tears in my eyes. Sports mean so much to Susan, but she seems to know that winning is not an end in itself. There are other things more important, among them kindness and fair play. She is such a satisfying daughter.

March 18, 1984

Our three eldest were baptized this evening at church, a moving occasion, and rather unusual to have three teens from the same family. Susan cried as she gave her testimony.

My deepest prayer always is that they will wholly follow the Lord, with single minds, not looking to the right or left; that they not be deterred by conflict nor distracted by the *things* of this world. Lovely as those things are, they will all perish. I pray that my children will set their sights on that treasure which is eternal.

Tonight was just one outward step in that direction. May there be many more.

March 28, 1984

The weather is unspeakable, rain all day with hints of snow.

Our old white Ford ('66) has over 250,000 miles on it and seems to get obstinate every cold morning. My patience has run thin. For the past three months we have chased around used-car lots looking for one that is (1) big enough for six people, (2) in good condition (Ed can sense trouble almost instantly), and (3) in our price range.

One night recently, Ed and the boys came home excited about a beautiful yellow Lincoln they had seen. A Lincoln? Yes, the Reads are now on the threshold of purchasing this lovely car, a huge one (1977) that will accommodate all of us comfortably. My book money, what was left of it, covered the cost exactly. God has his ways of supplying needs.

The kids are thrilled.

April 1, 1984

On Friday after school Anne came home and said she had accepted Jesus into her heart during reading class, where she and Faye Overly, her teacher, meet twice weekly for special instruction. That evening she told Ed. The next morning she reported it to Gramp when she went over for her private Saturday breakfast with him. It seems to be settled in her mind. Anne, with her little bright face, is like a flower that has just opened up in good soil.

At church today I spoke to Faye, who said she was reading aloud to Anne both John 3:16 and Romans 3:23. "Have you ever sinned?" queried Faye.

"Yes," was Anne's reply.

"And what is sin?"

Anne gave an apt answer. "Telling lies, like a shepherd who says he'll take care of the sheep and doesn't."

Faye talked a bit more, then asked Anne if she wanted to receive Jesus as her Savior. She did.

They prayed, Anne saying, "I know I have sinned, please forgive me." There were tears.

I believe she understands. She has peace. What a gift it is.

May 5, 1984

Just a week ago tonight we were in Missouri. Earlier Ed received a phone call that George, his brother, had died suddenly. The same day Ed made plans to fly out and had, in fact, bought the ticket when I got a brainstorm.

"We can *all* go for less than the price of the plane ticket," I said, "and with our big Lincoln, why shouldn't we? Maybe God had planned it that way for us. Please, could we go? The children don't even know the relatives."

I badgered and pleaded till Ed said yes. It sounded, well, awfully impetuous to him. That evening we flung ourselves together doing laundry, packing, making phone calls, and such. When we finally got to bed, Ed and I slept scarcely at all. At 2:30 a.m. we got up and left.

On trips Ed lets me drive as much as I want. The cruise control was such a help, taking off some of the strain. We arrived the morning of the second day just ten minutes before the funeral service.

And how wonderful that we went. George was a dear brother and we wanted to honor him. For the first time in their memory our children met Aunt Clara from Texas and Uncle Charles from Washington, not to mention spouses and cousins.

Families need to be cherished.

June 17, 1984

Having Irish relatives here is always one of our special pleasures. For three weeks we had James and Susan Hay from Galdonagh staying over at Mom and Dad's. We were back and forth between the two houses all day long. Susan and I had a great time shopping.

Temperatures hovered near 100 degrees for over a week,

giving them much more than a taste of American heat. It ended in a big storm the day before they left, and now it is delightful.

June 27, 1984

It is another pristine morning, too beautiful for sleep. I rise with Ed at six and have a long sit here at the table (possible since school is over) and a walk around the garden where I watch the dove feed her young. I'm finishing my study of Ezekiel this summer, noting the emphasis "that they might know that I am Lord." The great truth of life—with it there is sense and meaning and worth; without it all is blank, empty.

I am (with others) presently experiencing a most wonderful answer to prayer, part of the request for which I've prayed earnestly each Saturday the past two years and more. It is beyond expression, my relief and joy, though I pray on for further victories.

The goodness of God endureth continually.

July 21, 1984

We returned from a trip to New England on Thursday evening after a really happy six days. It will probably be the last family vacation. Next year James and Susan will both be working.

In Hampton, New York, we spent two nights with the Averys, warm, friendly folk who used to be part of our church. Then we went to New Hampshire, where Susie Britton and her family live in a beautiful, trendy house with a tower and circular staircase. It was nearly as good as staying in a castle.

Our favorite site was Newport, Rhode Island. There we

followed the cliff walk early in the day along the sea by all the mansions. One we toured was *The Breakers*, built by Vanderbilts, a big marble masterpiece, but hardly a place one could call *home*.

August 3, 1984

For two weeks we have Lakisha, a lively, little, black seven-year-old from New York City with us. I read Bible stories at night to her and Anne; she sits on the edge of her seat to listen. A bright, responsive child, she has been singing "Jesus Loves Me" off and on all day.

For my birthday Dad and Mom gave me a beautiful orange carpet for our living room. It has cheered the room dramatically, giving it a warm inviting look with the rockers and old-fashioned wallpaper. I like it now, bed and all.

Continuing answers to prayer these days. *O Lord, our Lord, how excellent is thy name in all the earth.*

September 17, 1984

Recently I've thought of all the unexpected ways God provided for us this year. Because it's easy to take blessings for granted, I must name them here. *Beware lest thou forget the Lord,* said Moses.

1. The return of Evelyn Bence into my life and the money I earned from some stories published in *Today's Christian Woman*.

2. An anonymous gift in January to each teacher in our school.

3. A gift in May that covered the reenrollment fee for all faculty children. These two gifts never came before, yet in what seemed to be a tight year they were provided.

4. In June the Petersheims phoned and said we could have all the strawberries we wanted, free, if we picked them. I got probably forty quarts.

5. The carpet from Mom and Dad which changed a dreary room into an attractive one.

6. A handmade quilt from Aunt Dee makes the bed blend in perfectly, all the right shades.

7. The reduction in tuition this fall for faculty children.

8. The work, painting and such, that Russell gave James and Susan at his rental houses, the lawns which the boys have cut; these jobs have enabled the three of them to buy all their own clothes.

November 13, 1984

There have been two historic days in our family this fall. The first, October 12, our glowing little Anne became a citizen of the United States. It was a happy occasion and especially so when Kim Taylor, her Korean friend, participated also. Afterward we had luncheon with the Taylors at the Landis Valley Motor Inn, along with fifty-seven other new citizens and families. It is wonderful to think that people still yearn to live in these United States, that they pay nearly any price to come.

Then on Saturday Mom and Dad celebrated their fiftieth wedding anniversary at Calvary Independent Church in Lancaster. We had food catered and Peg made a truly splendid cake.

What a singular heritage they have given us over the years. We can only rise up and call them blessed.

March 21, 1985

Big changes are in the air along with spring. Today I

picked up job applications at Shady Maple for James and Susan, who will both be able to work this summer. Can it be? My youngsters going off to work? Where have the years gone? As C. S. Lewis says, we must be made for eternity, else the flying years would not seem so strange. Fish don't remark on the wetness of water, yet people say, how time flies. Eternity is in our hearts.

James is learning to drive, but I've persuaded Susan to wait. One a year is enough.

The winter is over and it has been a turbulent one at school. I seem to have a headache at the end of each day.

But today I had my Bible Club here at home, with Peg Geiter's four children, Billy Powell, and my Anne. They're a happy enthusiastic little crowd, learning verses and listening carefully as I tell the Easter story, a segment each week. I'm also using Patricia St. John's *The Tanglewood's Secret*.

Susan has been knitting for the last months, her first attempt, a peach-colored baby sweater set, to submit at the regional competition in April. What persistence she has. I have no aptitude for that sort of thing and can't help her.

June 30, 1985

This year we have here for two weeks both Lakisha and her brother Kahim from New York. All I seem to do is cook. Everyone gets up in shifts, so I serve several breakfasts, with snacks and cups of tea all along for me. Ed turns up every couple hours from his job, looking for food. James leaves to work at Shady Maple Market, so he has early supper, the rest of us later. A good thing I like my kitchen. Susan will begin work soon.

I am reading the life of Hudson Taylor sent to me from long-ago friends in England, the Kendalls. I am moved deeply by his utter devotion to God and his burden for the people of China. In the book is a poignant story of a man called Nyi, who had long sought the truth, and his father before him. When he heard the message from Hudson Taylor, he became a believer in the Lord Jesus.

"How long have you had the glad tidings in England?" he asked Hudson.

The young missionary was ashamed to tell him, and vaguely replied that it was several hundred years.

"What!" exclaimed Nyi. "Is it possible you have known about Jesus so long and only now have come to tell us? My father sought the truth for more than twenty years and died without finding it. Oh, why did you not come sooner?"

There is no answer to that heart cry.

July 11, 1985

Neighbors, an older couple and one quite ill, have been on my mind (and in my prayers) very much recently. Today I stopped to see them. I said that I had been their neighbor since I was a little girl and I wondered if we would go on being neighbors in heaven one day.

"Did you ever accept the Lord Jesus into your lives?" I asked.

"No," they said.

"Would you like to?"

Their answer was no, clear and firm.

I talked a little longer and left some literature with them. I told them that I prayed regularly for them. And I came home. How joyless their eyes were, how drab their lives without that treasure which is Christ. Not to know him is unthinkable.

Anne—our favorite little allen, 6 years

Anne, sixth grade, 12 years

Anne, third grade, 9 years

Susan, 14, and Anne, 9, with Laddie

The Read children: Susan, Michael, Anne, James

Michael at 17

Susan at 18

James at 18

Our little white house at Narvon

Gram and Gramp Hay

Ed and Maureen Read

Ed doing what he enjoys!

Patricia St. John (Foreword writer) and her sister Hazel

August 26, 1985

This morning, early, I again committed my children to God, asking him to use them where and how he might see fit. There is always a certain fear. What if he asks them to do such, or go there, or give up even life itself? Am I willing for any of these outcomes? I tremble as I pray. Yet the only safe and joyful place is in God's will. May they seek it always.

The summer is nearly over. I went six times to airports, mostly to Kennedy and Newark, running a kind of shuttle service for various family members going to Ireland. I wonder when it will be my turn to go again.

September 19, 1985

The crickets, multitudes of them, are singing happily. The night is warm.

Yesterday at school one of my students was in tears over her cat's death. From the bus she had seen it smushed on the road. I tried fruitlessly to comfort her.

Today she told me cheerfully that it was a hapless rabbit flattened on the road. The cat was okay. "I had the cat for ten years," she said. "He's kinda like my *son*." I'm sure he is.

It is wonderful to see the new building going up at school. An extra asset is a couple, Manfred and Sharron Schneider from California, who traveled to Pennsylvania at their own expense to give us three months of help. Manfred is a master plumber, though he does other work as well.

We've had them at our place for dinner, warmhearted, friendly people. Ed has shown them some sights around the county, something he does well.

November 29, 1985

Michael was in his bedroom alone today again, having his quiet time, I believe. There's a quiet hunger for God in him. He reads his Bible daily, as well as other books, some profound. Lately I saw him with Hudson Taylor.

And I've been reading a biography of Amy Carmichael. This expresses what she does for me. "There is nothing so kindling as to see the soul of man or woman follow right over the edge of the usual into the untracked land, for love of Him, for sheer love of Him."°

January 12, 1986

The woods are snowy, dark, and deep these days.°°

Aunt Ruth, who still lives alone down the road, just called and said she has a mouse running all over her bed. I told her to look for a trap and set it. As I settled to read, she phoned again. She couldn't find a trap. James is now taking her two. He has always felt very kindly toward her.

It has been character-building for our youngsters to help her over the years. They have carried wood and coal to her in the winter, and cut grass and hedges in the summer. And they have learned the need to visit those who are elderly and lonely.

February 21, 1986

My manuscript, the one about Dad, came back this week after the publisher held it for over a year. I had had such hopes, especially after the editor phoned me en-

---

°From Mary Hatch in Frank Houghton, *Amy Carmichael of Doh-navur* (S.P.C.K., 1953), p. 302.

°°Adapted from Robert Frost, "Stopping by Woods on a Snowy Evening."

164

thusiastically last summer, but somehow the marketing committee is always the hitch. They want a guaranteed return on their investment.

I don't usually cry over rejections, but this time I did.

And still I remember my prayer and vow to God, that if nonpublishing is an acceptable sacrifice on behalf of the one for whom I pray, then I gladly give it, that that one might have the gift of faith and joy and strong assurance.

February 26, 1986

Aunt Ruth is finally moving. She cannot face another winter here on the hill by herself, coping with fires and loneliness, not to mention the thunderstorms of summer, of which she has always been afraid. She'll be moving to Fairmount Nursing Home after a sale at her place in June.

And the old post office, all these years in the spacious, old-fashioned building next door to us, is now housed in a brand-new, functional box down the road. Where else was there a post office with an enormous dusty moose head hanging in it? With a tin ceiling and pot-bellied stove, quaint scales, and an old ice box of 1928 vintage?

Only at Narvon. And now it is gone. Progress.

March 18, 1986

Such heartbreaking news came over the prayer chain. We are still reeling in shock. Little Kim Taylor, Anne's friend, has leukemia. How can this be? The Taylors have poured themselves into our school over the years and are greatly loved. *There is no searching of his understanding.*

She has had and will have extensive chemotherapy at Children's Hospital in Philadelphia, requiring months of uncertainty and pain.

School is out of joint with Mr. Taylor so preoccupied. There has been a massive outpouring of prayer for them.

June 10, 1986

Is there any joy quite like being at *home* on a June evening with school over and all the summer before me? The curtains are blowing on this lovely, clear evening. Tchaikovsky is on the stereo. Anne is happily copying 1 Corinthians 13, since we are memorizing that. I'm alternating between two favorite authors, and then the Scriptures themselves. *Thy testimonies have I taken as an heritage for ever: for they are the rejoicing of my heart. What* a heritage!

Ed took Anne and Mike to the circus at Hershey two weeks ago. At the last minute he said to me, "Why don't you go too?" It sounded so much better than staying home to clean as I had planned, that I dropped everything and went. It's nice to be wanted. We had a grand time together.

June 21, 1986

Today was the sale of Aunt Ruth's house and belongings. She was born in that house and lived there ever since with her parents and family until she only was left in the house. ,

As I walked down the road this morning, the last time ever to see her there, I wondered how *many* times I had gone there over the years. In my childhood it was a second home and I've visited there nearly every Sunday unless I was away.

I was fine till my cousin Nancy June came and we hugged each other and choked up. Memories of Granny's home fries and apple pies, of wood fires and kittens, of sitting on the porch on old rockers were in the very air.

It seems somehow indecent to display over the lawn all the accumulations of one hundred years of living: old dishes, postcards, a jelly cupboard, the bed on which all the children were conceived, a sideboard which for the first time today had no candy dish sitting on it for us to help ourselves.

A sweet kid chatted to me about some old money. Later his dad said he wanted the earthenware pie dishes. "Oh," I told him, "my grandmother made scores of pies in them that made my mouth water. I'm bidding too."

He understood. "I won't bid," he said. "My grandmother did that too. You take them."

So I came home with the pie dishes and Granny's rocker, where she used to sit and eat "coffee soup." Tonight the little house is empty after all those years of continuous living.

July 7, 1986

We are just back from Philadelphia Airport, where we left Hazel St. John after she spent a week with us. It was wonderful to be with her and recall the years together in Beirut, when she was my principal. Her influence has been great upon me. I am glad my children could know her. They have all read books by Patricia, who was prevented at the last minute from coming along with Hazel.

She has regaled us with stories of their active lives, two seventy-ish women with kids and teenagers in and out of their home all day, each one receiving bread and the Bread of life.

On Saturday our church choir, led by George Burdett,

sang a cantata at the New Holland Park. All six of us Reads were in it, Anne and Ed doing a special reading that pleased them both.

Afterward, I gathered up friends from the audience to come along and visit with Hazel: McConaghays, Betty Ann and her mother, Esther Palmateer and her children. We had a picnic tea on our front lawn as darkness fell. Those moments are always little preludes of heaven, a group that will never again be all together here, but there we will.

August 12, 1986

Summer runs along at a great rate, yet each day is a perfect, slow-motion, sleepy pleasure. The crickets and katydids have started dinning, beautiful but ominous sounds of fall.

Today Laurelyn, Eileen, assorted daughters, and I drove to Philadelphia Children's Hospital to see Kim Taylor, who has been there for a month of extended treatment, and her mother, Sue, who has also been there most of that time. It is a desperately sad and lonely place to be for such a length of time. I am ashamed that I hadn't gone sooner. The month passed so quickly for me. Fifty miles seemed such a way to go, and center-city a headache to negotiate. And so we only went today.

September 6, 1986

On Tuesday my nearest and dearest neighbor, Randy Fox, age 41, died suddenly. She was in her kitchen making chicken potpie and looked up and saw Jesus beckoning. Not long after, her mother found her lying on the floor while on the stove was the chocolate pudding burned fast.

What must it be like to be rolling dough and suddenly see him?

She was buried today in the Bridgeville Cemetery, very near Elizabeth.

October 12, 1986

Without him, God the Lord, how could anyone make it through life? There are so many burdens and heartaches to bear.

The most recent, and heaviest, came to our dear friends Sharron and Manfred in California. Their oldest son, Jeff, brilliant, hard-working, in love, has taken his own life. He left no letter, no explanation whatever.

His parents are desolate. What can one say? What comfort is there for such as this?

I've pondered much about it. There has to be more, much more than we can see, that whole unseen world of which the Bible speaks. Centuries ago God said to Satan, *Hast thou considered my servant Job ... blameless and upright, a man who fears God and shuns evil?*

And Satan said, *Does Job fear God for nothing?* He challenged the validity of Job's faith.

Then God permitted Satan to test Job. In the next verses Job lost his wealth, his family, his health. Even his wife told him to curse God and die. But Job's voice rings out over the centuries, *Though he slay me, yet will I trust him.*

Faith. It held fast.

And perhaps today God is saying of Manfred and Sharron, of the Taylors as they suffer with Kim, of Betty Ann in her lonely singlehood, of our dear friends, the McConaghays: "Have you considered them, Satan? They're mine. They'll pass the test."

And all the universe, that vast unseen world of the spirit, watches to see if a man or woman can have the kind of faith which clings to God even in the deepest sorrows of life, even when it seems to make no sense.

None of this do we see now, but only through a glass, darkly. One day we shall know. And then it will be worth it all.

November 22, 1986

A wonderful crisp bright day with towels blowing on the line and Laddie cheerfully watching as I hung them. And no neighbor-friend Randy ever out with her clothes anymore. A big emptiness there.

I've had nice reactions to my articles this month, especially "Homesick" in *Decision.* It seems as though most people are.

February 17, 1987

Life with teenagers is never dull. Today Mr. Taylor told me James is a finalist for the National Merit Scholarships. James was home, too sick to really care when I phoned him. He has been accepted by Wheaton College, a dream of his for a long time. And he had his first real date recently, the kind where you ask a girl ahead of time and take her out by yourself.

Susan is attending a Vietnamese church in Lancaster every other Sunday in a search for roots. It has been a bumpy year for her in school, but we are weathering it. She talks by the hour to me, about all these things. I've tried to explain that she is really between two worlds and will probably have to make a choice, one or the other. She is completely American in culture, education, family life, but her heritage is Vietnamese. She should treasure that, just as Gramp has his Irish heritage, but it is hard to cling to. For better or worse she is an American.

Her dream is to marry an Oriental and be a missionary, even in Vietnam. I wonder what God has for her. She is such a lovely girl.

Michael has played piano each Sunday for a month at Friedens, our mission church. He is reluctant to play in public, but plays by the hour at home with a fine sensitive touch.

Anne is not a teen yet, but she tries hard. Anything Susan does she wants to do also, sometimes with comical results.

February 23, 1987

It is thirteen years ago today that Elizabeth left us. I haven't wanted to cry till now, this evening. Yet she has been on my mind (and heart) today but without mourning. Just memories and a sense that There is very near.

Sharron Schneider wrote and her grief is fresh and piercing yet.

March 5, 1987

Spring is loitering somewhere, certainly not here. It's supposed to be warm by Saturday. That is when Ed will leave for Waxhall, N.C., to work on missionary pilot Dave King's new house. I commended him for giving up a vacation week and donating labor to such a project. He said simply, "Dave could probably earn $50,000 a year and more as a commercial pilot." Thus his own sacrifice seemed small to Ed, who has always admired Wycliffe people.

June 7, 1987

On Tuesday after supper I went across to see Mom. Dad was in Lancaster all day doing visitation for the church.

She wasn't in the kitchen and I felt a twinge of fear. It is so rare for Mom to be out of her routine. I walked on through to see if she was at the clothesline—and found her sprawled on the driveway. At first I saw only her legs and thought it was all over. Then I saw she was holding up her head watching the sky intently, the better to see the clouds and airplanes go by.

No, she didn't want an ambulance. She would get up with just a little help. But she couldn't.

The X-rays showed her pelvis is cracked in a couple places, so it will be a long healing. Will she ever walk again?

What a week it has been. The three big kids are in Arizona at a national competition, concluding with a weekend at an Apache Indian reservation. I was invited to go along but am so glad I didn't.

And in a couple weeks Anne Hay Thompson will be here from Ireland with her husband, Gerry, and four children. It is a busy time.

June 12, 1987

The first of three graduations in annual sequence took place last night for our family. James completed twelve years of education in our school and was valedictorian of his class. The theme of his speech was gratitude.

I didn't cry at all. That I had done on dark nights when I'd waken and fret about his leaving home. How could I send him, *any* of them, away? One is never rational in the wee hours.

And now Michael is learning to drive and has started to work at Shady Maple Smorgasbord along with the other two. I miss him sorely, his music, just his quiet presence. He has grown up with the least effort on my part, and I keep wondering if I've forgotten something along the way.

Early this morning I read in *Daily Light,* "Every thing that may abide the fire, ye shall make it go through the fire, and it shall be clean. The Lord your God proveth you . . . ."

I draw back instinctively, for the fire is so hot. Yet the Refiner watches the gold in the fire, watches until he can see his own face reflected.

May the proving bring out the best, himself, in our children as they begin to leave home.

June 24, 1987

Yesterday morning I ran across the road and found Dad having breakfast by himself. He was listening to the record of Rob Neff singing "Christ Is All." It was such a picture of Dad's life, that quiet morning time alone with God and the unshakable faith that Christ is all that matters.

I've been in the throes of cleaning both houses, Mom's and ours, and Anne has stayed by me when I needed her. She has learned to make Irish scone by herself and seems to have an aptitude for cooking. We have had some heart-to-heart talks, which work best when the other three are away at work.

Today Marie and Dewey were here to help in the final stages before the Irish guests arrive tomorrow.

Then Dad brought Mom home from the hospital and she is now set up in the living room with a room divider for some privacy. How she loved hearing the organ again and drinking tea and having Marie here, whose joy runs over. She sat in a chair, with Dad beside her holding her hand, the big one swollen ever since her surgery.

July 3, 1987

This must be my busiest summer ever. James is working ten-hour days for David Riehl, an Amish businessman, while Susan and Mike are still at Shady Maple on various shifts. Ed is moonlighting at odd jobs every evening. I serve supper and wash up from 3:00 p.m. when Ed eats, to nearly eight, when James finishes.

We are thoroughly enjoying the Irish cousins across the road. When they are here, I cook a meal for everyone, fourteen of us. Russell runs them around on tours many days, places like D.C. and Longwood Gardens.

All the teenagers have mingled well, talking about accents, outlook, clothing, driving. And Anne and I have renewed our friendship begun back in 1951, when we were both children in my grandmother's kitchen in Ireland. We had one carefree day, just she and I, at Park City.

July 20, 1987

Sitting outside in the humid dusk with fresh-picked blackberries on the table, I listen to all the sounds in the house. Upstairs James hums along with a concerto on his newly purchased Walkman as he sorts clothes for college. The three of them shopped today.

Anne roars around her room banging drawers as she gets ready to take a bath. She has not learned subtlety yet.

The sewing machine whirs as Susan shortens her new slacks. Michael plays his *Hungarian Dances* on the stereo.

The fans hum in several rooms. It's a hot night. Across

the road Mom begins to play the organ. Thank God, she is healing from her fall. Lightning bugs dot the darkness. Ed returns from a walk with the dog.

A July evening.

July 28, 1987

Michael passed his driver's test today, just like that. That was the good news. Then we stopped at Mellinger's and heard the bad news, that his insurance would be $1000 a year.

After some inquiry we found that if we put our old friend, the '66 Ford, into mothballs, it will be $600, still an outrageous amount, but manageable. He and Susan had a $300 bill on the Chevette this week. What expenses youngsters have these days.

Anne has been at camp all week, a wonderful respite for both her and me. She is so carefree and irresponsible and I seem to nag a lot. Am I too strict? Or am I really too easy? She is often out the door with her friends before I remember that her chores are not complete, that she's not practiced her music all week, that the dog has a hungry look about him.

I pray for wisdom often, that I might not scold too much, but that I'll not take the easy way either and spoil her.

She gets prettier all the time. Our least one is growing up.

August 22, 1987

I remember it clearly. On the way home from the hospital, we stopped to get a couple items of groceries. Ed ran into the store and I sat in the car looking at the small bundle in my arms, my first son, James. At that moment I thought, "Someday this little guy will be bigger than me and he'll grow up and leave home."

And that's what happened. Now eighteen and a half years later he's six feet tall and this week he went to college. We drove down the road together, Ed and I, this time with James driving, on our trip to Wheaton.

The years together of constant companionship flashed by me in those first few miles, pictures, vignettes of the past.

I saw him as a baby, hiccuping and fussy with colic. Would he ever learn to sleep three hours in succession? I saw him cutting his teeth on the edge of my shiny chrome teapot which he loved. The little marks are still there. And crawling, not in the orthodox way, but with a kind of purposeful yank forward on his elbows.

How proud and protective he was of his brother Michael and sister Elizabeth. When she went abruptly to heaven that dark night, he didn't cry, not then, but he said when the ground was white outside, "She's helping Jesus make snow 'cause she knows I like it." Later he did cry when he found the little scraps she had given him in his "office," a box where he kept his treasures. It was a heavy burden for a five-year-old.

I remember the first day of school. As soon as he learned to read, I heard very little from him. He read everything he could lay hands on and was an expert in American and English history by the time he was ten.

When Susan arrived from Vietnam, he took her to school with him. I stopped a few days later and heard him tell someone about "my sister." She belonged to him right from the start.

He was eleven when we went to the British Isles, and he knew well the stories of castles and palaces, of kings and queens. As we drove around London, he said, "Mommy, that looks like the Bishop's Palace over there." It was. I hadn't even known there was such a place.

A sensitive boy, he listened gladly to stories from the Bible each night. And it wasn't long until he read the Bible for himself, the Old Testament mostly with all the poetry, messages of strange and far-seeing prophets, stories of people and the glory of God. It builds character, the Old Testament does, and enriches the spirit. It improves one's English and is the beginning of wisdom.

When he was thirteen, he welcomed another sister, Anne. Before her arrival he said perceptively, "It will never be quite the same again." He has shown unfailing kindness and humor to her.

In recent years he and Michael ran across the road at 9:30 each evening and had tea with Gramp and Gram. A godly heritage, the greatest gift in life. Along with the tea and cookies, the scone and blackberry jam, they were served generous helpings of wisdom, stories from Ireland, Bible verses, encouragement, love, standards of right and wrong, much laughter. It was a place of safety in a world that seems to have few moorings left.

So much, so much to remember as we drive along the road. His frequent thanks to me for a good meal, his visits to Aunt Ruth in the nursing home, the diligent work in school, the classical music playing at full volume when he was alone or thought he was. I ache to think it's over.

His last morning he loitered in his room fiddling with the packing. He was in no hurry to leave, he said. He loved his room and had always been happy there. And so we waited for him. You can't scold a boy for not wanting to leave home.

Gramp and Gram, slowly with her walker, came across to say good-bye. It was brief. No one wanted to prolong it.

And then it was, as we drove down the road, that I began to remember all that the years had held. I looked at James. A dream of years, attending Wheaton College, was to be fulfilled. It was in many ways a miracle that it had worked out.

And yet another tear dripped from under his chin as he held the steering wheel. He was leaving childhood behind forever and it was bittersweet.

Epilogue

The years have gone, faster than a weaver's shuttle, as Job puts it, and our children seem perched on the edge of maturity.

Susan is now planning to go to Moody Bible Institute in Chicago, just twenty-five miles away from James at Wheaton. I can hardly believe the little brown girl I gathered into my arms all those years ago is big enough to leave home. What a dear daughter she has been to me.

We still have Michael and Anne at home, but not for long. Each day is precious, all the more for being so fleeting.

Before too long it will be just Ed and I—and Christ. Without Him the years ahead could look bleak, lonely, without purpose. With him we are just walking toward Home, in his company.

He has answered prayers, scores of them, over the years. How good is the God we adore.

The final prayer, as I send out this book, is for you as you read. We will probably never meet one another in this life, yet we can meet one day in his presence. And so, my first and deepest prayer for you is that you might *know* him, the only true God, and Jesus Christ whom he has sent. When you do, all else will fall into perspective and life will have joy and meaning. Jesus said, *I am come that they might have life, and that they might have it more abundantly.* What a gift is this!

For some of you, though, he is already your Friend and Savior. Yet you may have immense heartaches and wonder if he has forgotten you. I pray that you will know his healing touch and sense his presence even in the darkness.

Or in all the trials of life, you may have lost sight of him altogether, and grave doubts beset your mind, doubts about his goodness. Does he care? Does he hear? For you I pray that you will have the gift of faith renewed once again. Seek him and he will be found of you.

Whatever you need—eternal life, a healing of your heart, the gift of faith—he will give to you when you come to him humbly, as a least one.

The Author

Maureen Hay Read was born in Philadelphia. Her father, an immigrant from Ireland, and her American mother gave her and her brother a godly, stable home. When Maureen was seven, the family moved to Narvon, in Lancaster County, where she presently lives with her husband, Ed, and their children.

A graduate of Bryan College, Maureen has taught English in several schools, most notably for three years in a mission school in Beirut, Lebanon. She has done extensive travel in Europe and the Middle East.

For the past thirteen years she has taught at the Christian school sponsored by Twin Valley Bible Chapel near Morgantown, where she and her family attend services.

Maureen has written articles for magazines such as *Guideposts, Decision, Power, Moody Monthly, Today's Christian Woman, Sunday Digest.* Her first book, *Like a Watered Garden,* published by Herald Press/Guideposts, has sold over 190,000 copies.